# STAINED
# GLASS

# STAINED GLASS

## AN ILLUSTRATED HISTORY

## SARAH BROWN

CRESCENT BOOKS
NEW YORK/AVENEL, NEW JERSEY

# ACKNOWLEDGEMENTS

Numerous friends and colleagues have provided advice, information and assistance in the preparation of this book; their help has improved it immeasurably, although errors can only be laid at my door. I would like to thank in particular Peter Cormack and Martin Harrison, without whom no history of Gothic Revival and Arts and Crafts stained glass can be attempted. I am also grateful to David O'Connor, Christopher St. J.H. Daniel, Professor Rudiger Becksmann, Ivo Rausch, Dr Erhard Drachenberg, Joan Vila-Grau, Professor Caterina Pirina, Dr Hilary Wayment, Alfred Fisher, Theodore Ziolkowski and Dr Stefan Trumpler, who have all assisted in the provision of illustrative material. A number of practising stained-glass artists have courteously responded to enquiries about their own work and have helped me to contact other artists; Rodney Bender has been particularly kind in this respect. I have greatly appreciated the patient help of my editor at Studio Editions, Alison Effeny, and the efforts of Lesley Coleman who has been tireless in pursuit of illustrations. On a personal note, I would like to thank Sue Pitt for her unfailing enthusiasm and interest, and Susan Mathews, who has so patiently taught me the rudiments of glass-painting and glazing, considerably improving my appreciation of the skills of the glass-painter, medieval and modern. Finally, I would like to thank my parents for their love, encouragement and support in everything I have embarked upon.

First published in Great Britain by Studio Editions Ltd
Princess House, 50 Eastcastle Street,
London W1N 7AP

This 1992 edition published by Crescent Books, distributed by Outlet Book Company, Inc., a Random House Company, 40 Engelhard Avenue, Avenel, New Jersey, 07001

Printed and bound in Singapore

ISBN 0-517-06967-9

8 7 6 5 4 3 2 1

**Title page** A newcomer to stained glass, Benjamin Finn's startling and imaginative compositions are already exciting critical interest. *The Spirit of God Moving over the Waters* (1990) evokes the words of Genesis 1:2.

# CONTENTS

# THE ORIGINS OF STAINED GLASS

Glass is an ancient material. Even before man had found a way to manufacture it at will, he had discovered the useful properties of its naturally occurring forms. The volcanic material obsidian, for example, could be chipped and fashioned into implements and weapons. As early as the Palaeolithic period (3,500,000–5000 BC), arrowheads and spears were made in this way. Relatively light, hard and brittle, obsidian was widely used wherever volcanic activity had taken place.

The origins of man-made glass cannot be dated with precision, but at least 3,000 years before the birth of Christ it was known to the cultures of the Eastern Mediterranean. Glass is made by combining silica (sand) and an alkali (ash), which when heated together form a homogeneous substance. Writing in the twelfth century, the monk whose pseudonym was Theophilus advised that the sand and ash mixture be heated for a night and a day. Impurities in the sand and metallic oxides deliberately added to the molten mix caused the glass to become coloured. Two basic types of ancient glass are known. That familiar to the Romans was made by the combination of sand and the ash of sea plants, which produced a material often described as 'soda glass' that was relatively durable and resistant to decay; fragments excavated at Jarrow (Northumberland) dating from the late seventh to ninth centuries have retained their translucency after centuries of burial. From about AD 1000 onwards, woodland ash (Theophilus recommends beechwood) was more commonly used, producing a glass rich in potassium and thus more susceptible to weathering and decay. The two traditions of glass production certainly overlapped and co-existed, but by the thirteenth

**Above** An extraordinary variety of glass objects, some functional and some decorative, have survived from Ancient Egypt. This glass fish, excavated at Tel el Amarna, is made of contrasting glass threads, moulded together and combed into a marbled pattern.

**Opposite** In his *History of the Abbots*, Bede describes the glazing of the seventh-century monastery church of Jarrow by Frankish glaziers, of which a conjectural reconstruction is shown here. The Christian Church, for which stained glass had such a special meaning, was thus responsible for reintroducing a lost craft to Anglo-Saxon England.

century woodland glass predominated.

This technical shift no doubt reflected the move away from coastal sites of glass manufacture, where the glass-house was close to the supply of sand, towards forested glass-house sites with easy access to the wood which served both as a source of raw material and as fuel. Theophilus' recipe for the manufacture of glass requires two-thirds ash to one-third sand, and a woodland site offered clear advantages.

Probably the earliest and certainly the best-known literary account of the invention of glass is that of the Roman historian Pliny the Elder (AD 23–79). In his *Historia Naturalis* he drew upon earlier Greek sources and described how Phoenician sailors camping on the shores of the River Belus (the River Naaman in Israel) rested their cauldrons on lumps of soda over a fire constructed on the sandy shore: 'when these became heated and were completely mingled with the sand on the beach, a strange translucent liquid flowed forth in streams; and this, it is said, was the origin of glass'.

Numerous glass objects and vessels have survived from the Egyptian world, and despite Pliny's account, modern scholarship has suggested Egypt as the country of origin of man-made glass. In 1370 BC the Pharaoh Thotmes established a glass industry at Tel el Amarna and excavations there have recovered evidence of glass production on a considerable scale. The earliest artefacts and vessels were produced by moulding and pressing the still malleable material into shape. Mosaic dishes of great beauty and sophistication were made by the fusion in moulds of sections of coloured glass rod. At an early date, cold glass was being cut, abraded and engraved.

The great revolution in glass technology, that is, the introduction of the blowpipe, which allowed far greater manipulation of malleable glass, cannot be dated, or indeed geographically located, with any precision. It is now thought that the blowpipe first appeared in the middle of the first century BC, and, like the discovery of glass itself, its original use was probably a matter of chance. The earliest evidence for glass-blowing has been found in

**Below**  The volcanic eruption of Vesuvius in August 79 AD froze a moment in time for the prosperous Roman town of Pompeii. A wide range of mouth-blown glass vessels were found among the many artefacts.

**Left** The transparent quality of glass made it a popular and challenging subject for depiction in the still-life wall paintings in Roman villas. This mural, showing a deep bowl brimming with fruits, was found in the house of Julia Felix at Pompeii.

Israel and Syria. Mouth-blown vessels could be mass-produced, and this same technology was eventually applied to the manufacture of glass suitable for windows. Use of the blowpipe became widespread in the course of the first century AD. Numerous mouth-blown glass vessels in a variety of shapes and colours were buried at Pompeii by the eruption of Mount Vesuvius in August 79 AD and some were recovered from the cemetery there, having been buried with the dead of an even earlier age. A number of villas had still-life paintings on their walls which included depictions of glass vessels.

It was the Romans who first fully appreciated the enormous potential of this material, light, impermeable, cheap to produce, which did not impart a taste to substances stored in it. Its use was no longer confined to decorative and luxury purposes; it became a material with a functional role. Glass vessels were used to export goods throughout the Roman Empire – glass could be blown into square moulds to create shapes that were easy to pack for transportation, like those of the late first century AD now in Colchester Museum. Not until the Industrial Revolution of the late eighteenth and early nineteenth centuries did glass come to be so widely used as it was in the Roman world. Middle Eastern craftsmen were attracted to Rome, where by the third century glass-makers constituted a sufficiently significant section of the population to attract taxation. The use of glass spread throughout the Empire, creating a demand which in turn stimulated the establishment of glass industries in other parts of Europe; there is evidence of activity in the valley of the Po, in Gaul, the Rhineland (especially Cologne) and even in the belatedly colonized British territories (London, Colchester and Wroxeter). Although the Romans were the first to use glass for purely functional purposes, their craftsmen were also responsible for some of the finest works of art in glass, including, of course, the Portland Vase and Lycurgus Cup, both in the British Museum. The Portland Vase, recently subjected to intensive scrutiny while undergoing conservation and proven to be a free-blown vessel (that is, not blown into a mould), is now dated as early as 30–20 BC and has been attributed to the artist Diosourides, who was

**Above** The Portland Vase is acknowledged to be one of the finest, and certainly the best-known surviving Roman glass vessels. Close scrutiny during recent conservation has proved it to be a mouth-blown vessel of blue flashed glass.

commissioned to engrave gems for the Emperor Augustus.

It is perhaps surprising, therefore, that the use of glass in an architectural context was slow to emerge. Windows in Roman buildings, particularly those of high status, were sometimes filled with glass, but it was only one of a number of materials, including mica, alabaster, shell and waxed linen, which were set into decorative frames of wood, plaster and even bronze. The earliest window glass was cast rather than blown and the individual pieces were small. Molten glass was poured into trays lined with sand and left to cool. Many fragments bear the imprint of the tray on their surface. The use of these windows of *claustra* or *transennae* was widespread in the Roman and Muslim worlds. Fifth-century alabaster examples were found in the church of San Apollinare in Classe in Ravenna. In Italy they continued in use into the eleventh and twelfth centuries (in Torcello Cathedral and San Cataldo in Palermo, for example).

In northern Europe, where there was less sunshine, glass with its greater degree of transparency was a far more practical choice, although where money was scarce, cheaper materials were used. Bishop Wilfrid's church in York, for example, originally had windows filled with linen cloths and pierced slabs which he replaced in about 670 with glass. The introduction of grooved strips of strong yet malleable lead as a matrix for the glass pieces was to prove the second crucial technological advance. The date on which this innovation first appeared remains unclear, although fragments of glass in lead have been found in the remains of Roman secular buildings at Trier (Germany) and Senlis (France).

Although window glass was used in domestic contexts from an early date, it was its employment in Christian churches that was to secure its future and foster its development as a decorative art. Its appeal to the Church was as much spiritual as it was aesthetic. In the book of Genesis we are told that God's first act after the creation of Heaven and Earth was to divide the light from the darkness (1:4). His first words are *Fiat Lux*, 'Let there be Light' (1:3). 'And God saw the Light, that it was good'. In the New Testament this theme is elaborated ; in St John's Gospel, Christ is called *Lux Vera*, the True Light, and in the same book Christ twice describes himself as the 'Light of the World' and the saved as the 'Children of Light'. Thus a material, which besides serving a functional purpose also played a decorative role and admitted light to the interior of a place of worship, was assured success.

The literary evidence for the early use of decorative arrangements of coloured glass in the windows of churches is plentiful. The Spanish poet Prudentius (348–c.410) admiringly described the 'glass in colours without number' that he saw in the windows of the basilicas in Constantinople. St Sidonius Apollinaris (c.324–c.480), Bishop of Clermont, mentioned the multicoloured figures in the glass windows of the basilica of the Maccabees, and St Gregory of Tours (c.540–94) lists those Merovingian churches with glass windows.

It emerges very clearly in Gregory's sixth-century *History of the Franks* and Bede's eighth-century *History of the English* that it was the Church that helped preserve many of the cultural, artistic and technical achievements of the Romans during the turbulent centuries after the fall of the Empire and the emergence of the new European kingdoms. Very few domestic buildings were glazed in this period, and according to Bede's *Historia Abbatum* (*History of the Abbots of Monkwearmouth*), the craft of glazing had died out completely in Anglo-Saxon England. In 675, Abbot Benedict Biscop, who had travelled widely on the Continent and had even visited Rome, imported Frankish craftsmen to glaze his newly established church at Monkwearmouth. In England it was thus the Christian Church that was directly responsible for the revival of a lost craft. Excavations in 1969 on the Monkwearmouth and Jarrow sites recovered complete quarries of window glass and a number of coloured fragments dating from the late seventh to ninth centuries. As no traces of paint were found on these fragments, it has been suggested that the outlines of the design depended solely on the pattern of the lead cames, examples of which were also discovered.

It is not known when paint was first applied and fired onto window glass, for it is the combination of coloured glass and painted detail that is the essential characteristic of stained glass. Archaeological evidence has now provided us with a considerable corpus of early painted glass. During the restoration of the church of San Vitale in Ravenna in the early years of the twentieth century, a number of glass fragments were found at the base of windows believed to be from the sixth-century cloister. The majority of pieces were unpainted, but a single fragmentary disc of glass bore traces of paint depicting Christ in Benediction. In 1878 several glass pieces and a fragment of grooved lead were recovered from a cemetery abandoned in about 1000 at Séry-les-Mézières in France. These streaky green and yellow fragments formed a cross with the Alpha and Omega symbols. These

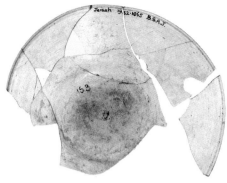

**Above** This fragment of crown glass and a plaster *transenna*, found in Jordan, illustrate one of the commonest alternative methods of glazing a window without lead cames.

**Below** This cloudy disc of glass, thought to have originated in the mid sixth-century cloister of San Vitale, in Ravenna, depicts Christ flanked by the Alpha and Omega. It has been suggested that it was held in place in a plaster *transenna*, although window leads have also been found.

**Above** This striking head, acquired for the Musée de l'Oeuvre Notre Dame in 1923, probably came from the abbey church at Wissembourg, on the Rhine. Dating from c.1060, the head is remarkably similar in style to that from Lorsch.

**Right** Lorsch-an-der-Bergstrasse was a royal abbey founded in the eighth century. The fragmentary head of a saint (probably ninth-century) was found in a debris-filled ditch in 1935.

valuable fragments were destroyed in the First World War, but not before they had been photographed. Originally identified as part of a reliquary, in 1966 they were recognized by the stained-glass historian Jean Lafond to have been painted window glass and have been attributed to the ninth century.

Literary evidence for glass-painting can also be found from the ninth century onwards. In the *Life of St Liudger* (d.809), bishop of Munster, written in 864, a pilgrim at the shrine is described gazing at images painted in the windows. The fragmented ninth-century head of a saint from Lorsch is the sort of image that the pilgrim might have seen. In the late tenth century Archbishop Adalberon of Reims (d.989) is recorded as having presented the church of Saint Remi with '*fenestris diversas continentibus historias* (windows containing diverse stories)', revealing that at an early date the narrative and instructive potential of stained glass had been appreciated. Perhaps the most interesting and personal description of a gift of painted windows is contained in a letter from Abbot Gozbert of Tegernsee in Bavaria (928–1001), thanking Count Arnold von Vohburg for his generous gift of stained glass: 'Thanks to you, for the first time the sun shines with golden rays on the pavement of our basilica, passing through varicoloured painted glass'. Until this time the church had only linen cloths at its windows.

In the course of the eleventh century many of the greater churches were glazed with painted glass. The beautiful eleventh-century head of Christ preserved in the Musée de l'Oeuvre Notre Dame in Strasbourg already displays the kind of three-stage tonal painting described by Theophilus a century later. The earliest painted glass to survive in an architectural setting is the set of four monumental prophet figures of *c.*1100 preserved in Augsburg Cathedral. The assurance with which they are conceived suggests that their creators were drawing upon a well-established artistic and technical tradition, an assumption shared by Theophilus' almost contemporary treatise. It is against a technical and artistic tradition of centuries that the Augsburg prophets should be viewed.

**Above** The prophet Daniel, one of four surviving figures of *c.*1100, was made for one of the upper windows of the eleventh-century Cathedral of Augsburg. Twenty-two figures survived until the seventeenth century, part of a series representing the Heavenly Jerusalem.

# THE GLASS-PAINTER'S CRAFT

The high cost of the materials used in the manufacture of a stained-glass window means that the glass-painter's craft has always been highly prized. It is no coincidence that Abbot Suger applied the terminology of gemstones to the 'sapphire blue' glass used so abundantly at St Denis. The high value of stained glass is further demonstrated by the reuse of so much of it in new buildings, in which it must often have looked old-fashioned in a more recent setting. The best-known example of this salvage and reuse is the famous 'Notre Dame de la Belle-Verrière' in Chartres Cathedral, but other examples could be cited. In York Minster, for example, late twelfth-century panels were saved from the demolished Norman choir and west work and were reused in the clerestory windows of the fourteenth-century nave, where their antiquated style was less evident when viewed from the floor of the nave.

## THE MIDDLE AGES AND THE RENAISSANCE

Suger's definition of the value of his windows did not rest solely on the monetary value of the raw materials, however. The workmanship of the glass-painter was equally appreciated. It is, in fact, important to stress at the outset that the medieval artist-craftsman who made a stained-glass window was not normally responsible for the manufacture of the coloured glass used. In the Middle Ages glass was purchased, as today, from a merchant middleman who dealt directly with the glass-houses which produced glass vessels as well as sheets of glass suitable for glazing. The activities of the glass-house can be seen in an early fifteenth-century Bohemian manuscript

**Above** In Jost Amman's *Panoplia Omnium Artium* (*Book of Trades*), published in Frankfurt in 1568, the glazier (on the left) leads up a panel of bull's-eyes. His grozing irons can be seen lying on the end of his bench. On the right the glass-painter works on a piece of glass propped up against the large window of his studio.

**Opposite** This early fifteenth-century manuscript illumination of *The Travels of Sir John de Mandeville*, probably from Bohemia, depicts a medieval glass-house at work. Although the glass-blowers are concentrating on glass vessels, the techniques illustrated here were common to vessel and window glass manufacture.

of Sir John de Mandeville's travels. Bohemia has supported an important glass industry since the Middle Ages. The glass-house depicted is situated close to a plentiful supply of sand (silica) and the wood which provided both a fuel for the kilns and one of the raw materials (ash) for glass-making.

The molten glass mix was 'cooked' in clay pots into which a variety of metallic oxides could be introduced to impart colour, giving rise to the description of these coloured glasses as 'pot-metals'. Two types of window glass were produced in the Middle Ages. The more common was the cylinder or muff, in which the bubble of malleable glass taken up onto the blowpipe was manipulated into a cylinder. This was then cut open along its length, gently reheated and pressed flat into a sheet with characteristic raised edges. In the alternative crown method, the bubble of glass was transferred from the blowpipe to a 'pontil' iron and spun so that centrifugal force caused the open-ended balloon to flatten into a round crown, thicker at the centre than at the edges. The 'bull's-eye' at the centre would not normally be used for the highest quality work, although glass was too costly for it to be discarded entirely. Jost Amman's sixteenth-century craftsman's handbook shows bull's-eyes being leaded into domestic windows. Their lumpy shape was sometimes used also in figurative panels where a 'sculptural' effect was sought.

Red glass (called ruby) presented the glass-maker with some problems. Pot-metal red glass is so dark in colour that little light can pass through it. The solution was to dip a gather of white glass into a pot of red and work the two together. The result was a 'flashed glass', in other words a laminated glass, a layer of red on a layer of white. In the second half of the thirteenth century glaziers began to abrade the ruby surface of the flashed glass to reveal the white glass beneath. One of the earliest examples of abrasion is to be found in ornamental glass of c.1260 from the Cistercian monastery of Schulpforta in Germany, while in the first quarter of the fourteenth century this technique is employed to depict the whites of the eyes of a ruby demon in the church of St Ouen in Rouen. The teeth of the early sixteenth-century

**Above**  This small panel of ornamental glazing of c.1260 from the Cistercian church of Schulpforta in Germany, contains at its centre an extremely early example of the technique of abrading ruby flash to reveal the white base glass beneath.

**Right**  Modern glass-blowers at work. The firm of Hartley Wood in Sunderland, founded in 1893, is now the only company in Britain producing mouth-blown antique glasses for stained glass. The muffs of glass, here shown being made in 1991, would have been familiar to any medieval glass-maker.

**Left** Peter Hemmel's magnificent St Catherine, made c.1480 for Kloster Nonnberg in Salzburg in Austria, is dressed in a damask gown of abraded ruby glass in an intricate design. The left-hand philosopher's sleeves are also abraded out of ruby flash.

Leviathan at Fairford in Gloucestershire are precisely abraded, as is the refined damask robe of St Catherine painted in about 1480 by the workshop of Peter Hemmel, now in the Hessisches Landesmuseum in Darmstadt. In the later Middle Ages, other colours of flashed glass, blue, for example, were produced, although ruby remained the most common.

The finished sheets or crowns of glass were purchased by weight rather than area. A variety of terms is found in medieval documents. The English 'wey' or 'wisp' weighed approximately 2.25 kg (5 lb) and the 'seam' consisted of twenty-four weys (approximately 54.4 kg or 120 lb). Coloured glass was more costly than white; English glaziers were generally paid twice as much for coloured, which was imported from Europe, as for plain, which was made in England. For the royal glazing at St Stephen's Chapel, Westminster, in 1351–2, the price differential was even greater. White glass from Chiddingfold (in Surrey) cost 6d per wey, red 2s 6d and blue 3s.

The contribution of the glass-maker should not be underestimated in an appreciation of a stained-glass window. Mouth-blown glass (known today as 'antique') has a texture and life absent in modern machine-made glass. In medieval glass the uneven texture is further emphasized by variations of tone and hue caused by bubbles of air and chemical impurities present in the raw materials used. Glass-making was anything but a precise science.

The most valuable source of information on the making of a medieval window is to be found in the late twelfth-century treatise *De Diversis Artibus* (*On the Various Arts*), by the German monk who adopted the pen name of Theophilus. Theophilus does, in fact, include an account of how to make a muff of glass, but the most useful part of his treatise concerns the work of the glazier and glass-painter rather than that of the glass-maker. Many of the techniques described by Theophilus would be equally familiar to the modern glass-painter.

Central to the design and manufacture of a medieval window was the

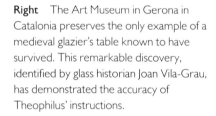

**Right** The Art Museum in Gerona in Catalonia preserves the only example of a medieval glazier's table known to have survived. This remarkable discovery, identified by glass historian Joan Vila-Grau, has demonstrated the accuracy of Theophilus' instructions.

glass-painter's whitewashed table. In an age in which paper was scarce and vellum and parchment extremely expensive, it was impractical to attempt to produce the kind of full-scale working drawing (called a 'cartoon') from which the modern stained-glass artist usually works today. Instead, the scaled-up design, sized to fit a template taken from the actual window opening, was drawn in charcoal at full size onto a wooden trestle table coated with chalk or whitewash. The drawing was marked with letters or symbols to indicate the colours of the individual pieces of glass to be used, together with the principal painted lines and highlights. This 'master drawing' thus served as a guide for both the glass-cutter and the glass-painter and doubled up as a workbench for the assembly and leading-up of the completed window. The recent discovery of two sections of a fourteenth-century table at Gerona Cathedral in Catalonia in Spain dramatically illustrates a process hitherto known only from Theophilus. One section shows a design for a canopy with leaf crockets and finial, drawn out using ruler and compass. Colours are indicated, together with the painted detail on one leaf. The design is crisscrossed with the holes left by the nails used to hold the individual pieces of glass in place during leading.

**Left**  The mid fourteenth-century stained-glass canopy made from the Gerona table.

**Right** The fourteenth-century clerestory windows of Tewkesbury Abbey employ a limited number of cartoons. In this window, on the north side, the first and fourth figures have been created from the same cartoon, although they were made up in reverse to give the impression of variety.

The whitewashed table was a tremendously practical working tool. Its use explains a great deal about medieval design procedures, for while cheap and easy to use, it was not readily portable and could not easily be stored as a means of preserving a design, as a modern paper cartoon can be. A full-scale design was, however, frequently used more than once in a medieval glazing scheme; at Tewkesbury Abbey in Gloucestershire, for example, the prophet figures are derived from only three or four basic figure models. This kind of reuse, often with slight adaptations or even simply reversed, is almost always confined to a single glazing scheme. All those canopies, figures or heraldic devices sharing a table were presumably produced in quick succession. Accounts for the glazing of St Stephen's Chapel, Westminster, in 1351–2 include payments for beer for washing the tables. An ultraviolet examination of the Gerona table has revealed the shadows of more than one design. The modern cartoon, in contrast, often has a long life. A large nineteenth-century firm would use a popular design many times over a long period.

A recent detailed study of a number of early sixteenth-century panels produced in Troyes in Champagne has shown that designs originally thought to have been taken from a single 'cartoon' in fact represent the reinterpretation, with adjustments and adaptations, of a workshop 'model' perhaps preserved in some kind of workshop sketchbook. Medieval sketchbooks are known to have existed; the late fourteenth-century Pepysian sketchbook in Magdalene College, Cambridge, contains images added over quite a long period and one folio (17$^v$) bears the outline of a window tracery, prompting the suggestion that it was a sketchbook in a glazier's workshop.

The exact nature of the design process is a difficult one to unravel.

Theophilus implies that the craftsman glass-painter was also the designer. In many cases this must certainly have been so. In other circumstances, however, the patron supplied the artists with sketches from which to work. In 1447 the English glass-painter John Prudde was given 'patterns of paper, afterwards to be newly traced and painted by another at the charge of the said glasier' to serve as models for the stained glass of the Beauchamp Chapel, Warwick. As these patterns required 'translation', it is clear that they were small sketches rather than full-size 'cartoons'. In the 1490s the glass-painters engaged to provide stained glass for the church of the Observant Friars at Greenwich were given precise written instructions, complemented with small sketches to show the correct appearance of the heraldry. In other instances, it is clear that the glass-painters were involved in a creative dialogue with the patron. Sketch designs preserved in Brussels, thought to have been produced for Cardinal Wolsey's chapel at Hampton Court in the early sixteenth century, offered the patron a choice between two versions of the Crucifixion. The design for another window also attributed to Wolsey's patronage, now in Edinburgh, was probably made by a German artist called Erhard Schön, but once in England was annotated with suggestions for alternative arrangements, thought to be in the hand of the glass-painter James Nicholson.

It is not known exactly when paper cartoons were first used by

**Above** Ultraviolet examination of the lower part of the Gerona table revealed the shadow of an earlier design, of the Virgin Annunciate, with hand raised.

**Above** The figure of the Virgin from the Gerona table executed in stained glass.

**Left** St Jan's church in Gouda preserves the most complete set of paper cartoons to have survived from pre-Reformation Europe. It is thought that these finely detailed and well-preserved drawings were hung in the studio to guide the glass-painters.

**Right** This early sixteenth-century drawing of an enormous thirteen-light window has been annotated at the top by the glazier, possibly James Nicholson, to suggest to his patron alternative arrangements. The *vidimus*, meaning 'we have seen', provided a kind of visual contract between patron and glass-painter.

glass-painters. The earliest documentary references relate, not surprisingly, to fourteenth-century Italy, to Siena Cathedral in 1355. Paper was more readily available in Italy than in Europe north of the Alps. The advantages of the reusable cartoon were clearly appreciated – a small mid fourteenth-century parchment cartoon of St Catherine survives from Seitenstetten in Austria. The cost and limited size of sheets of parchment would have restricted the use of this material. Even sheets of paper were too small for a full-size cartoon. Cennino Cennini, writing of Italian practice of the late fourteenth century, describes how sheets of paper should be glued together to make cartoons. The relatively early availability of paper cartoons in Italy may well explain the relative frequency with which Italian artists supplied cartoons for glass-painters. Cennini suggested that 'those masters who make [stained glass] possess[ed] more skill than draughts-manship' and so were forced to turn to other artists for the creation of the cartoon. This was no doubt greatly facilitated by the use of paper which could be rolled up and taken back to the glass-painter's shop with ease. The earliest surviving Italian cartoons are those for the architect Pellegrino

Tibaldi's window for the nave of Milan Cathedral, made by Corrado de Colonia in 1567 and preserved in the Pinacoteca Ambrosiana in Milan. Without doubt, the most impressive series of cartoons to survive are the sixteenth-century paper cartoons for the windows of St Jan's church in Gouda, in the Netherlands. Made in the years after 1555, these cartoons were deposited by the artists with the church authorities in order that authoritative repairs could be made when necessary. There is no evidence that these cartoons were ever used on a bench in the way that the glazier's table would function; rather it has been very plausibly suggested that these remarkably finely worked drawings were hung in the studio to serve as a guide to the painters, for they do not supply the 'cut-line' guide essential for the glass-cutter.

The Gouda cartoons provide evidence that the introduction of paper affected the way in which the glass-painter worked. The primacy of the glazier's table was undermined, and successful and popular designs could be reused time and time again. In addition, the design process could now take place outside the glass-painter's studio. A comparison of a small panel depicting St Augustine in Nuremburg with a cartoon in Erlangen shows that an artist could produce a design allowing for a number of variations; here the design permits either a quatrefoil or medallion treatment and the border of the finished panel is rather simpler than the one envisaged by the designer.

Documentary sources reveal that by the early sixteenth century paper was widely used for cartooning stained glass. In 1503 the will of the York glass-painter Robert Preston bequeathed 'all my scrowles' to Thomas English, while in 1508 John Petty left his 'scoes' to his brother Thomas. An inventory of the workshop of the Parisian glass-painter Laurent Marchant made in 1579 records 'several large cartoons on paper which were used to make church windows'.

**Below** In translating this early sixteenth-century design of St Augustine in his study by Hans Suess von Kulmbach into glass, Veit Hirsvogel has simplified the border and has added a label at the base of the panel.

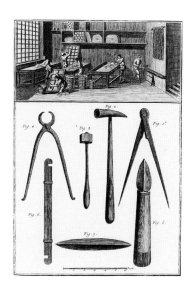

**Above** Diderot's *Encyclopédie* of 1751–72 illustrates the glazier's tools, including the straight grozing iron at bottom left. At the top, glaziers are shown milling lead, cutting glass and making clear windows.

**Right** The face of the Virgin Annunciate of *c.*1340 from Hadzor in Worcestershire (now in the Stained Glass Museum in Ely Cathedral) admirably demonstrates the effectiveness of strong trace-lines.

With the 'cut-line', the colour of glass to be used and the main painted details established, the first step in the realization of the window was to select and cut the glass required. The medieval glazier cut glass by the application of a heated iron to its surface. The roughly cut pieces were then trimmed into shape with a 'grozing iron', with a hook at each end, which left a characteristic 'nibbled edge'. No medieval grozing irons have survived, but they are frequently mentioned in documents. At Windsor in 1351, Simon le Smyth was paid 1d each for 'croisures'. They are depicted in glass in a shield of the Glaziers Company in the York parish church of St Helen, and can be seen in Jost Amman's illustrations of the glazier's workshop. Extraordinarily complex shapes were cut using this relatively crude method and the grozing iron is still illustrated amongst other glazier's tools in Diderot's *Encyclopédie* of 1751–72, by which time the diamond cutter was in use. This tool had appeared in Italy by the fourteenth century and its use became widespread in the course of the sixteenth. It left a straight edge, and the ease with which regular shapes could be cut made it invaluable for cutting large numbers of diamond quarries for plain glazing.

After the cutting of the glass came the most skilful operation of all: the painting. Glass paint, called 'geet' or 'arnement' in English documents, was made of iron or copper oxide (Cennini mentions copper filings), ground glass, gum arabic (to help the paint to adhere to the surface of the glass before firing) and a binder like water, wine, vinegar, or even urine. The paint, which can vary in colour from grey-black to brown, could be diluted to a variety of consistencies depending on the effects sought. An india-ink consistency was suitable for the basic trace-lines, a thinner wash for modelling purposes. Brushes were made from a variety of animal hairs, including sable, squirrel and badger. Sticks, needles, quills and even fingers

**Left**  The finest heads in the early fifteenth-century east window of York Minster, like this one of Edward the Confessor, demonstrate John Thornton's mastery of a number of different painting and modelling techniques.

were also used to manipulate, texture and scratch out the paint to modify its effect on the light passing through the glass. Even the lightest application of paint affects the quality of light transmission. Most paint was applied to the interior surface of the glass, although it could also be applied to the exterior (called 'backpainting') in order to reinforce the main painted line or to create a particular effect – the river water washing around the legs of St Christopher, for example. On the interior surface, the main outlines were painted in thick trace-lines, with highlights taken out of a thin overlying layer of paint (called 'matting'), which was smoothed to an even texture with the use of a badger-hair brush. In English this process is called 'badgering'. 'Smear-shading' with thin washes of paint could be used for shadowed areas such as eye-sockets, and from the mid fourteenth century 'stipple-shading' was used to create a softened modelling by dabbing the paint with the bristles of a hard brush. By using different binding media, the glass-painter could place one type of painted detail alongside another without them running into one another. The only alternative to this would be to fire each stage in the painting, a time-consuming and potentially dangerous proce-

**Right** The Annunciation to Joachim (c.1340–50) from York Minster demonstrates the wide range of tones possible when using yellow stain. Joachim's collar is a fine example of stick-work and scratching-out.

dure, for each time a piece of glass is fired there is the risk of it cracking.

Apart from the black or brown glass-paint, the only other pigment known to the medieval glass-painter that could be applied with a brush was yellow or silver stain. A solution of silver nitrate or oxide (the St Stephen's Chapel accounts mention silver filings) was introduced to the glass-painting repertoire some time around the year 1300. The earliest firmly dated example is probably in a window of 1313 in the parish church of Le Mesnil-Villeman (Manche) in France, where it is used to colour white glass yellow and blue glass green. The technique is also found in England in the 'Heraldic Window' in York Minster datable to c.1307–10, and it is far more likely that it was an innovation first developed in one of the great metropolitan glass-painting centres. Like glass-paint, yellow stain must be fired onto the glass to make it adhere permanently. Its colour can vary enormously, from a pale, lemon yellow to a deep, brassy orange.

Theophilus describes the construction of a kiln for firing painted glass. It was a simple structure, made of clay and constructed over a frame of arched twigs. In order to fuse the painted decoration onto the surface, the glass must be fired at a temperature of at least 600–650°C. It has been estimated that a wood-fuelled kiln would take about six hours to reach the desired temperature and about twelve hours to cool. Modern kilns are thermostatically controlled, but the medieval glazier had no such technical assistance and must have relied on experience and the appearance of the glass as it reached the firing temperature. Yellow stain is fired at a lower temperature than glass-paint and so is applied after the initial painting and first firing.

Theophilus mentions a further embellishment available to the glass-painter. He describes how glass 'jewels' can be applied using a thick layer of glass-paint: 'paint a thick colour between them [the jewels] so that none of it runs between the two glasses. Then fire them in the kiln with the other parts and they will stick so firmly that they will never fall out.' 'Annealed' jewels of this type are found in glass of c.1230 in Regensburg Cathedral (Germany) and in fourteenth-century glass at Klosterneuberg in Austria. Unfortunately, Theophilus' confidence in this technique was misplaced, for in many cases the 'jewels' have become displaced, leaving blank patches behind them, as in fifteenth-century glass in St Michael, Spurriergate, in York.

The leading-up of the panel brought together the individual painted, stained and fired pieces of glass, uniting them into a meaningful mosaic of colour and painted detail. The leading-up was done on top of the drawing on the glazier's table, and sorting marks scratched in the glass-paint before firing helped the glaziers to reunite the pieces that belonged together. Grooved strips of lead of varying thickness (called cames) were cast in H-sectioned moulds by the glaziers themselves. The moulds are described by Theophilus. Medieval leads, which survive in surprising numbers, sometimes have pin-prick holes in their heart, where bubbles of air have been trapped in the mould during casting. From the sixteenth century onwards lead mills came into use, producing longer, thinner and more supple leads, although medieval cast leads seem to have been more durable. Window lead is normally estimated to have an effective life of 100 to 150 years.

The lead does far more than simply hold the glass in place. Although its

**Left** At St Michael Spurriergate in York, early fifteenth-century annealed 'jewels' like those described by Theophilus have been used to decorate an oval halo. One has become detached (bottom right), leaving a white patch on the glass.

**Above** During conservation in 1976–7 this small early fourteenth-century panel depicting the stonemason William Campiun was found to be in its original medieval leads. The lead was too weak to be reused, but clearly shows how the designer had carefully integrated it into the image.

aesthetic role in a medieval window has often been obscured by later repairs, it was fully integrated into the original design, carrying the principal outlines of the composition and strengthening the painted line. Great care and skill were employed to ensure the correct and effective positioning of the leads. The joints of the leaded panel were soldered and the whole panel had to be waterproofed on both sides. An oily cement was forced under every leaf of the lead and into every joint. Only then was the window ready to keep out the elements.

The ferramenta, the iron-work set into the window opening to support the weight of the glass, was provided by a smith rather than the glazier, although it was the glazier's responsibility to ensure that the glass was fixed accurately and securely into the window. In lancet windows of the twelfth and thirteenth centuries the ferramenta could be extremely complex, providing an elaborate and decorative framework for the panels of glass. Only when the scaffolding was removed was the glazier's responsibility over.

## THE SEVENTEENTH AND EIGHTEENTH CENTURIES

Around the middle of the sixteenth century, a new range of vitreous enamel pigments that could be painted onto the surface of white glass was discovered. Like basic glass-paint and yellow stain, these enamel colours had to be fired to make them permanent. The earliest coloured stain (after yellow stain) was a reddish haematite-based colour called 'Jean Cousin' or 'Cousin's red' after its supposed inventor, the sixteenth-century Sens glass-painter of that name, although it was in use from the middle of the fifteenth century. This colour was used sparingly to add a naturalistic blush to lips and cheeks, for example, and can be seen on some early sixteenth-century windows, such as those in King's College Chapel, Cambridge. Thereafter, green, blue and purple enamel colours were introduced. These relied on glass as a raw material, for all used ground glass as a flux. They proved very helpful to glass-painters called upon to create increasingly complex heraldic displays; enamels freed them from the necessity of cutting tiny pieces of glass that required separate leading. Initially, therefore, enamel stains are found complementing traditional glazing techniques.

Enamels were also used to great effect on small-scale panels, roundels and medallions intended for domestic settings. Enamel colours lack opacity and are less effective when viewed in great expanses from a distance. They were, however, ideal for delicate detail on small panels that were to be viewed close up. A glass-painter could imitate the easel painter, working on a single sheet of white glass rather as the painter works on a canvas.

The widespread use of enamel stains also undermined the traditional approach to the use of lead. There was no longer any need to cut glass into intricate shapes, and glass-painters began to work on large, regular rectangles of white glass. Lead was still required, for there was still a technical limit to the size of the individual sheets of glass and too large a piece would break when placed in a window. Many enamel-painted windows are composed on a regular grid of glass and lead, giving the rather disconcerting impression of viewing a scene through a grille.

**Left** The Conversion of St Paul, painted in enamel stains on large squares of white glass by Joshua Price, after a painting by Sebastiano Ricci, was made c.1712–16 for Bulstrode Park in Buckinghamshire. It is now in the church of St Andrew-by-the-Wardrobe in London.

## THE NINETEENTH AND TWENTIETH CENTURIES

All of the techniques described by Theophilus would have been familiar to the glass-painters and glaziers of the nineteenth century. The revival of stained glass at this period was fostered by a determination to restore the traditional skills of the Middle Ages. The apologists of the Gothic Revival revered the craftsmen of the past and a close study of their work was essential to the recovery of the technical intricacies of the craft.

One of the most serious obstacles to the creation of stained glass in an

**Above** This bottle from the studio of Christopher Whall, now in a private collection, is one of the few surviving slab-glass bottles that provided the thick, uneven, but brilliantly coloured glass favoured by the artists of the Arts and Crafts Movement.

authentic Gothic idiom was the poor quality of glass available to the glass artist. The intellectual and aesthetic evolution of the Gothic Revival in stained glass is discussed elsewhere, but as important as the cultural factors were the technological advances that supported the artists and designers. Experimentation in glass technology took place almost simultaneously in France, Germany and England, as the ingenuity and perseverance of the Industrial Revolution were brought to bear on stained glass. As early as 1802, Alexandre Brongniart, director of the Sèvres factory, was experimenting, unsuccessfully, in medieval methods of glass-making, and in 1828 the factory opened a stained-glass workshop. In 1826 the chemist Gustave Bontemps had succeeded in manufacturing a ruby glass coloured throughout. In Germany, the patronage of the eccentric Ludwig I of Bavaria was instrumental in the founding of the Munich State Workshop in 1827. Perhaps the most successful experimentation, however, was to take place in England. Here the impetus was provided not by a chemist, but by the barrister and stained-glass historian Charles Winston (1814–65), whose studies of medieval glass and encouragement of contemporary artists led him to appreciate that no true revival was possible with inferior raw materials. In 1849 he enlisted the help of Dr Medlock of the Royal College of Chemists in the analysis of samples of medieval glass. Edward Green of the London firm of James Powell and Sons of Whitefriars Glass Works was engaged to make the new glass that resulted from the experiment. This was used for the first time in the restoration of the fourteenth-century stained glass of Bristol Cathedral Lady Chapel, undertaken by Joseph Bell of Bristol under Winston's supervision. In 1863 William Edward Chance of Birmingham also perfected an 'antique' glass.

Although glass-painters of the nineteenth century prided themselves on their recovery of traditional skills, they were quite prepared to take advantage of appropriate technological advances, many of which had been made in the manufacture of table glass. Flashed glasses could be etched very effectively by exposing the coloured flash to the action of acid, the areas of colour to be retained being protected by a 'resist' of wax. Acid etching was in fact known to the late medieval glass-painter; Antonio da Pisa's late fourteenth-century technical treatise mentions 'goldsmith's strong water'. It was not widely employed in the Middle Ages, however, although it has now become a basic and widespread technique. Hydrofluoric acid is used and a range of acid-resistant films are now employed to mask the areas to be protected. Acid etching allows for a wide range of effects, and a flash can be progressively removed to create a graduated diminution of colour.

A further important technical innovation of the nineteenth century also concerns the manufacture of glass. In 1889 the Southwark firm of Britten and Gilson developed a thick slab glass known as 'Prior's Early English' after the architect E.S. Prior, who first suggested it. The new product was made by blowing a bubble of glass into a mould designed specifically to create a square glass bottle, which was then split into four sides and a heavy base. The resulting slabs were extremely thick and uneven in texture, but were intensely coloured and gave a brilliant and gem-like effect. 'Norman slab', as this type of glass came to be known, is difficult to cut and lead because of its considerable and uneven thickness, and windows made of slab glass have a distinctive lumpy exterior surface. Slab glass was used extensively by the artists of the English Arts and Crafts Movement, for whom it became a craft hallmark. It is extremely costly and is no longer produced, so that surviving supplies of it are eagerly sought.

Another range of new glasses deserves mention. Although they were also extensively used for lamps and table wares, they are strongly associated with stained glass and represent a specifically American contribution to the medium. Two figures stand out – John La Farge (1835–1910) and Louis Comfort Tiffany (1848–1933), praised at the Paris Exposition Universelle of 1900 for his 'dumbfounding versatility'. Tiffany's first patent for opalescent glass was registered in 1881, and in 1892 he established the Corona glass furnace on Long Island and formed the Tiffany Glass and Decorating Company. Thenceforward, Tiffany's windows were made exclusively of his own spectacular 'Favrile' glasses. The sheets of glass were hand- and machine-rolled into irregular sheets from as many as seven ladles of different coloured glasses, creating a bewildering variation of iridescent tones. 'Fractured' or 'confetti' glass contained chips and fragments of coloured glass embedded into sheets of clear glass. So great were the variations of colour within a single piece of glass, that paint was dispensed with altogether. Variations and intensification of colour can also be achieved by plating one piece of glass on top of another. The Irish stained-glass artist Harry Clarke used this technique extensively, together with both acid etching and staining.

The twentieth century has also contributed a range of new techniques. One of the most important has been the *dalle de verre*, used for the first time in 1927 by the Parisian glazier Jean Gaudin. The glass *dalles* (slabs) are cast in moulds and are 4 to 5 cm (1½ to 2 in) thick and approximately 30 cm (1 ft) long. Used without paint in a mosaic-like manner, they are incised with a cutting wheel and then tapped sharply against an anvil or other angled

**Left** Gabriel Loire's *dalle de verre* windows for the First Presbyterian church in Stamford, Connecticut, introduced this twentieth-century technique to America.

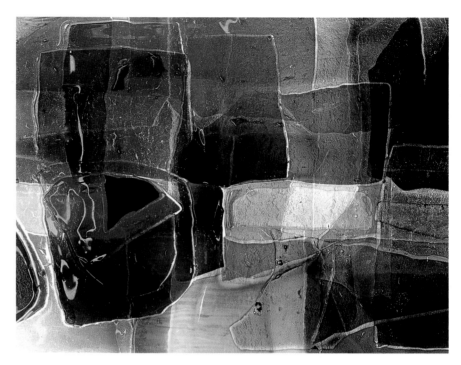

edge. A variety of tungsten-tipped hammers is used to shape the pieces of glass, which are formed into chunky shapes and are also struck on their surface to create a lively, faceted effect. The pieces are laid out as required by the design and a frame is placed around them to create a mould. Cement or epoxy resin is then poured into the spaces between the *dalles*. If cement is used, metal braces must be placed between the pieces of glass to provide the cement with reinforcement. With resins, which have the advantage of being lighter, no extra strengthening is required.

After hesitant beginnings, *dalles de verre* enjoyed considerable success in the 1950s and 1960s, when they were recognized as being particularly appropriate to the architecture of reinforced concrete. The technique has been used to considerable effect in structures such as Gabriel Loire's glass for the First Presbyterian church in Stamford, Connecticut and in the lantern of the Roman Catholic Cathedral in Liverpool by John Piper and Patrick Reyntiens.

Techniques suitable for small-scale projects include glass appliqué and fusing, both of which are based on collage. In appliqué, as its name suggests, coloured pieces are bonded to the surface of a clear base using an adhesive. Unfortunately, many of the adhesives used have been found to discolour and break down in sunlight, and appliqué panels are unlikely to have a long life, although the technique has proved popular for small domestic panels and screens. Fused glass combines layers of different coloured glasses by the application of intense heat. Not all types of glass are suitable for this sort of work and strong natural light or artificial back-lighting is required for the best results. The effects achieved can be very rich and interesting.

The high cost of coloured and antique glasses has encouraged considerable experimentation with the substantially cheaper machine-made flat glasses now available. Flat glass has little life or surface texture, but can be acid-etched or sand-blasted very effectively. Sand-blasting can be used as a

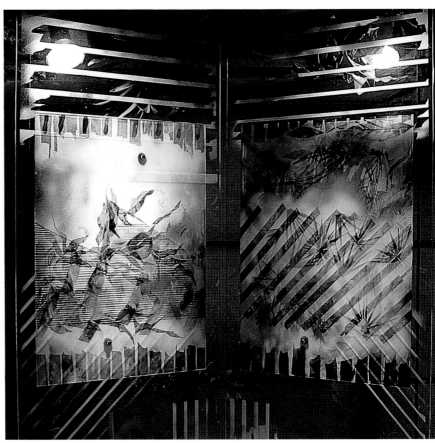

**Right** Jane McDonald's screen employs the iridescent lustres more commonly associated with ceramic decoration.

safer alternative to aciding. As in acid-etching, the areas to be left plain are protected with a resist and the exposed surfaces are then subjected to a powerful stream of silica particles. The coarseness of the particles and the length of time the particle stream continues will affect the end result. The effects can range from a slight clouding to a deep cutting of the surface.

The range of commercially produced glass-paints, stains and vitreous enamels available to the modern glass-painter is extensive. To the repertoire of more conventional glass-painting pigments can be added a selection of metallic lustres, more usually applied to ceramics to give an iridescent finish. Lustres are generally all fired at the same temperature, allowing several colours to be fired together.

Lead remains the perfect material for bonding stained glass, although other materials have been used. Max Ainmuller's 1855 windows in the chapel of Peterhouse College, Cambridge, are made of iron, for example. In modern windows zinc, brass and copper can be found, although all are less easily bent to shape than lead and so are best suited to designs using straight lines.

One of the greatest differences between medieval and modern practice lies in the cartooning of a window. As we have seen, the glazier's table was superseded by the paper cartoon in the course of the sixteenth century. This facilitated the commissioning of designs from artists in other media and could transform a glass-painter's work. The late eighteenth-century York glass-painter William Peckitt was a poor draughtsman on the evidence of figures that can be directly attributed to his hand, although for many of his commissions he used cartoons drawn by the artist Biaggio Rebecca. In the nineteenth century, one of the most remarkable examples of the separation of the design from the execution of a window occurred in the firm of Morris and Company. Edward Burne-Jones produced large numbers of cartoons for the company – after 1874 he was the firm's chief stained-glass designer – but decisions as to colour and often as to background motifs were made by William Morris, and the actual painting was entrusted to a team of expert glass-painters. Many of Burne-Jones's cartoons were reused over a long period and some even served as the basis for work in other media; the angels in stained glass at Salisbury Cathedral reappear in tapestry at Brockhampton church in Herefordshire, for example. Glass-painters of the nineteenth century were quick to make good use of photographic techniques; many designs of this time were enlarged photographically from small drawings to full-size cartoons, reducing quite dramatically the time and effort normally involved in the cartooning process.

From the cartoon the glass-painter must also produce a cut-line drawing, which, as its name suggests, shows exactly how the glass is to be cut and where the lead lines are to be positioned. The cut-line will also reveal any technical inconsistencies in the design which can be adjusted accordingly; it is numbered and marked with the colours of the glass to be used.

In France and Germany the cut-line itself is then cut up to provide templates for the shaping of the individual pieces of glass. A special pair of double-bladed shears, which take out a strip around 2 mm or one-sixteenth of an inch (i.e. the normal thickness of the heart of the lead) between each piece of the template, is used. This ensures that the pieces of glass to be cut from the templates will allow for the width of the leading in the finished panel. The glass can then be cut following the edges of the templates, and the pieces reassembled in a frame. Melted beeswax is poured between the pieces, so that when set it can serve as a temporary matrix holding the glass together and allow it to be painted in a state as closely resembling the complete window as possible. The painting can be done vertically against the light or horizontally with the waxed panel resting on a lightbox. When painted the panel can easily be disassembled for firing and leading.

In Britain the cut-line is used rather differently. Glass is cut by placing it over the drawing and following the cut-line visible beneath. The preserved drawing is then traced onto a sheet of plate glass, with the lead lines thickened and darkened to the correct widths. The pieces of glass are transferred to the plate-glass sheet and held in place on its surface by plasticine blobs or by beeswax introduced into the spaces between them. The plate can then be hoisted onto an easel and viewed against daylight. Any discordant colours can be altered and painting can begin. This method recreates a kind of glazier's table, although the modern version, taking advantage of the large sheets of clear glass available through present-day glass-making techniques, enables the glass-painter to work on his whole panel against the light. The medieval artist, working on a wooden table, would not easily have been able to gauge the overall effect of his work. Given the limitations imposed on him, our admiration for his skill and judgement must be all the greater.

# ROMANESQUE: STAINED GLASS IN THE TWELFTH CENTURY

And let the brush strokes be thick in one place, light in another
and then lighter, and distinguished with such care that they give
the appearance of three shades of colour being applied.

So writes Theophilus in his craftsman's textbook *De Diversis Artibus* (*On the Various Arts*), written in the first quarter of the twelfth century, the period from which stained glass begins to survive in appreciable quantities. 'Theophilus' was the pseudonym of a German Benedictine monk, possibly the metalworker Roger of Helmarshausen, the creator of a reliquary which survives as part of a portable altar in Paderborn Cathedral. Although the longest section of the treatise is devoted to metalworking, a considerable part (Book Two), discusses every aspect of the construction of a stained-glass window and reveals that by the beginning of the twelfth century stained glass was a well-established craft throughout medieval Europe. France was already renowned for her stained glass – Theophilus refers to her 'precious variety of windows'. Much has been lost; William of Malmesbury, for example, wrote in glowing terms of the earlier choir of Canterbury, consecrated in 1130 and destroyed by fire in 1174: 'Nothing comparable was to be seen in England, either for the brilliancy of the windows, the splendour of the marble pavement, or the ceiling with coloured pictures'. Theophilus wrote his treatise in a German abbey and it is particularly appropriate, therefore, that the earliest surviving image of a glass-painter is of German origin. Preserved in the Landesmuseum in Munster in Westphalia is a panel of Moses and the Burning Bush, one of five

**Above** The Presentation in the Temple from the Infancy of Christ window at St Denis (c.1145), is one of the best-preserved of Suger's original panels. Important vestiges of the St Denis glazing have been in the parish church at Twycross (Leicestershire) since 1840.

**Opposite** The Flight into Egypt, now in the Glencairn Museum, Bryn Athyn (Pennsylvania), is also from the St Denis Infancy window. The window was removed from the abbey in 1799, many of its panels were broken and some were sold in 1802 to the English dealer John Christopher Hampp.

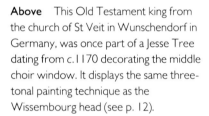

**Above**  This Old Testament king from the church of St Veit in Wunschendorf in Germany, was once part of a Jesse Tree dating from *c.*1170 decorating the middle choir window. It displays the same three-tonal painting technique as the Wissembourg head (see p. 12).

**Above right**  At the base of a panel of *c.*1160 depicting Moses and the Burning Bush, the artist Gerlachus is represented in the earliest surviving image of a glass-painter. This panel, originally made for the Premonstratensian abbey of Arnstein an der Lahn, was probably once paired with the Annunciation to the Virgin Mary.

**Opposite**  Hosea, King David and Jonah from Augsburg Cathedral. Together with Daniel (see p. 13), these four figures of *c.*1100 are thought to be the earliest surviving *in situ* glazing. The fifth figure, of Moses, was made during a sixteenth-century restoration.

survivors made *c.*1160 for the choir of the Abbey of Arnstein an der Lahn by the glass-painter Gerlachus, who appears at the base of the Moses panel.

The windows of twelfth-century churches are relatively small, simple, round-headed openings in the thick-walled structures necessary to hold up the vaulted roof above. The stained glass which filled them was thus designed to admit as much light as possible, although corrosion of the surface and simple dirt can often darken the glass so that its original effect is distorted. Those Romanesque windows which display least deterioration and disturbance reveal that at their best they were bright and jewel-like, with a high proportion of light glass. The colour described by Abbot Suger of St Denis (1081–1151) as 'sapphire blue' is balanced by lighter blues, a pale purple, rich greens and gold. A sparkling white provides a counterpoint to these brilliant colours.

Examination of early twelfth-century glass-paintings confirms that Theophilus had a first-hand knowledge of the glass-painters' techniques. The head, probably of Christ, from Wissembourg in Alsace (now in the Musée de l'Oeuvre Notre Dame, Strasbourg), painted in *c.*1160, clearly demonstrates the three tones of painting which he describes (see p. 12). There is some hint of plasticity in the modelling of the features, but the head, with its severe frontal arrangement, large eyes and strongly linear treatment of the beard and hair, is an essentially flat, two-dimensional image. There is an ornamental symmetry in the painting of the nostrils and the ears and even the furrows of the brow create a decorative effect. An almost identical painting technique was employed to the same effect on the

head of an Old Testament king from the church of St Veit, Wunschendorf (Germany), painted in about 1170.

A fascination with linear pattern used in an abstract manner is one of the hallmarks of Romanesque painting. The monumental impact of this style is perfectly demonstrated by the four figures, Daniel, Hosea, David and Jonah, in Augsburg Cathedral dating from c.1100, almost exactly contemporary with Theophilus' handbook. (The fifth figure, of Moses, is a sixteenth-century addition.) The richly dressed figures, set off against a background of clear glass, are conceived as flat blocks of colour. Their draperies are modelled with thick black lines which seem to pull the cloth in tight, angular creases, particularly on the shoulders, where the drapery almost resembles fish-scales. Knees are suggested by formalized spirals, while the palms of their upheld hands are painted with rigid, parallel striations and their feet rest on fleshy palmettes (although Jonah's have already disappeared into the mouth of the whale).

Stained glass of the first half of the twelfth century is relatively scarce, and consists of single figures and scattered panels rather than extensive schemes. The austerely frontal, seated Virgin and Child in the church of the Holy Trinity at Vendôme (second quarter of the twelfth century) exemplifies the abstract quality of Romanesque figure drawing. The figures are conceived as a lozenge-shaped grouping, the angularity of the pose emphasized by the closely painted parallel lines of drapery, which cascade across the legs of the Virgin Mother in pointed V-shaped folds. This treatment of the human form as a kind of flat plane of conventionalized decoration is characteristic of the best Romanesque art.

A rhythm of a different kind is set up in the panel of the Ascension from Le Mans Cathedral (c.1140). The Apostles and the Virgin Mary are grouped like swaying dancers, balancing on undulating mounds beneath their feet. Their gestures, which lead the eye upwards to the Ascending Christ (now lost), are emphasized by the artificially regular lines of their draperies and the matched symmetry of their positioning against alternating blocks of red and blue glass.

Poitiers Cathedral has three windows which are almost perfectly preserved in situ. The Crucifixion and Ascension window of c.1170 was the gift of King Henry II of England and his wife, Eleanor of Aquitaine, who appear at the base of the window. This window effectively demonstrates the flat, abstract approach to the conception of the devotional image. The figure of the Crucified Christ, with eyes open, is emphasized by his size, for he towers over the figures standing on his left and right. His arms are stretched out against a red cross which almost entirely fills the width of the window and which is itself emphasized by the scalloped blue and gold beaded border. The spear and vinegar sop held by the flanking figures of Longinus and Stephaton lead the eye towards his wide-eyed suffering face and the posture of all four figures at the foot of the Cross serves to draw the eye inwards. The figures, dressed in blues, purples and greens, are silhouetted against a red panel. The arms of the Cross serve to divide the upper tier of the window into two compartments, crammed with the upward-pointing Apostles and the Virgin Mary, who witness the Ascension at the apex of the window. Christ is conveyed into Heaven in an almond-shaped mandorla supported by the swaying figures of two angels, whose figures are unnaturally arched inwards to fill the space available and to emphasize the figure of Christ.

The designer of the Poitiers window has selected two key incidents from the Life of Christ to serve as the culminating devotional icon for a glazing scheme at the east end of the Cathedral. For windows dedicated to a more detailed exposition of the Biblical narrative or for the narration of the Lives of the Saints, a different approach was adopted, exemplified by the three windows in the west wall of Chartres Cathedral of c.1150, windows which escaped the fire of 1194 that resulted in the reconstruction and reglazing of the rest of the church in the Gothic style. Cleaned in 1975–7, these windows are remarkably legible, depicting the Infancy and Passion of Christ and the Tree of Jesse. The window opening is divided into a series of

**Above** The Virgin and Child from the abbey church of La Trinité in Vendôme, painted in the second quarter of the twelfth century, displays extreme stylistic formalization. The Virgin Mother is here represented as the aloof Queen of Heaven, in contrast to the tender humanity of later images (see p. 71).

**Left** The Apostles and the Virgin who witness the Ascension (c.1140–5) in Le Mans Cathedral, are probably the earliest surviving examples of French stained glass.

**Far left** This striking little figure in the diocesan museum at Klagenfurt in Austria is thought to have originated in the baptismal chapel of St John and St Mary Magdalene in the church at Weitenfeld. Made c.1160–70, St Mary Magdalene carries a pot of ointment, her most usual attribute in medieval art.

compartments, some circular, some square, sometimes used in alternation (as in the Infancy window). The individual compartments are separated by rich bands of foliage enclosed in beaded borders of white glass. Thus the separate episodes can clearly be distinguished. The figures within them are large, entirely filling the available space. Hands and heads (some restored) are large, and gestures, so important to the successful narration of the stores, can be clearly read. Despite the enormous number of figures portrayed, the compartments provide a structure to the whole and prevent it from dissolving into confusion.

The west windows of Chartres are heavily indebted to the windows of Abbot Suger's newly built church of St Denis (1140–4), now acknowledged to be one of the most important artistic monuments of the twelfth century, although its fame was no less great at the time of its creation. The prestige of St Denis, and thus its stained glass, rested on its close associations with the French Crown. The abbey had been founded in the seventh century by King Dagobert in honour of St Denis and his companions Saints Rusticus and Eleutherius. It housed the tombs of the founders of the Capetian dynasty. In 1127 St Bernard (c.1090–1153), the founder of the Cistercian Order, acknowledged this special status when he wrote to Suger: 'This place has been distinguished and of royal dignity from ancient times'. Suger (c.1081–1151), whose origins were relatively humble, had met the young Louis le Gros (Louis VII) early in his career when the young king was at the abbey for his education. He rose to become abbot in 1122 and during the king's absence on the Second Crusade he was made regent of France, earning the title 'Father of the Fatherland' on the king's return.

**Right**   The Infancy of Christ in the west wall of Chartres Cathedral (c.1145–55) is one of the most extensive narrative cycles of its kind. It is also the earliest example of regularly alternating compartments, enhancing the legibility of the window.

The rebuilding of St Denis was the culmination of Suger's 'reform' of the abbey and was intended to consolidate its claims to pre-eminence. Now recognized as an early experiment in the Gothic style, St Denis is an architectural monument of international significance, befitting its religious and political importance. Suger recorded the process of reconstruction and beautification in two books – *Liber de rebus in administratione sua gestis* (*On what was done under his administration*) and *Libellus alter de consecratione ecclesiae Sancti Dionysii* (*On the consecreation of the church of St Denis*). These books provide valuable information on the original glazing conceived for the new church and provide proof, if any were needed, that Suger himself was the intellectual author of the scheme. Little is said of the glass-painters, although we are told that the windows were 'painted by the exquisite hands of many masters from different regions'. The windows were highly valued for 'their wonderful execution and the profuse expenditure of painted glass and sapphire glass', and accordingly an official master craftsman was appointed for their protection and repair.

It is clear that the stained glass was considered to be an important aspect of the abbey's decoration. Suger describes the scheme as commencing with the Tree of Jesse in the chevet and also mentions by name windows with scenes of St Paul, the unveiling of Moses, the Ark of the Covenant, a symbolic window, the unsealing of the Book by the Lion and the Lamb and scenes from the Life of Moses. The glass of St Denis has suffered enormous damage and depredation. Because of its associations with the monarchy, a great deal of damage was done during the French Revolution, when the glass was removed and much of it lost. Only Suger's aisle windows remain, the upper glazing levels having been destroyed during later building campaigns. Although extensive restorations were carried out in the nineteenth century, not all of the dispersed glass was returned to the church and panels are now to be found in other churches and museum collections round the world. The remaining panels in St Denis now contain a great deal of nineteenth-century repair and restoration, although the prestige of Suger's writings has meant that a high proportion of the glass he mentions by name has survived, albeit in a restored state.

To those windows listed by Suger can be added windows depicting the Infancy and Passion of Christ (together with the Jesse Tree, copied at Chartres), a window of Ezekiel's visions, a Life of the Virgin Mary, the Lives of St Benedict and St Vincent, a window depicting the First Crusade (a panel of which survives in the Glencairn Museum, Bryn Athyn, Pennsylvania) and a Charlemagne window (panel also at Bryn Athyn). At the feet of the Virgin of the Annunciation is the recumbent figure of Suger himself (only the head of the figure is now in original twelfth-century glass). A second 'portrait' of Suger offering a window appears at the foot of the Jesse Tree, although this is now entirely of nineteenth-century date.

The Chartres glaziers rushed to imitate Suger's glass as soon as the west wall of their new nave was ready to receive stained glass. Thus, the Tree of Jesse which in St Denis was positioned in the east end, in Chartres is found at the west. Although the Tree of Jesse (a depiction of Christ's genealogical descent from Jesse) was not a subject invented by Suger, the St Denis

**Above** The Crucifixion and Ascension are brought together in a single window of c.1170 in Poitiers Cathedral. The designer avoids narrative confusion by using contrasting coloured compartments into which the figures are placed.

**Right** King Josias from Canterbury Cathedral is one of two surviving panels from a Jesse Tree of c.1200 made for the Corona chapel of the Cathedral. The Canterbury panel is extremely well preserved, unlike the slightly earlier York example.

**Opposite** The York Minster Jesse Tree panel (c.1170–80) was made for the Romanesque choir of the Minster, swept away by the reconstruction of the late fourteenth and fifteenth centuries. The Romanesque panels at York are now attributed to the patronage of Archbishop Roger of Pont L'Eveque.

window made it a popular subject for late twelfth-century stained glass; Roger of Pont L'Eveque, archbishop of York, commissioned one for his Minster c.1170–80, for example. The St Denis Jesse would certainly have been known in England, Queen Eleanor of Aquitaine had been present for the consecration of the St Denis choir in 1144 and may have influenced the decision to install a Tree of Jesse at the east end of the new choir of Canterbury Cathedral, which she visited in 1194. Both the York and Canterbury Jesse Trees owe aspects of their design to the St Denis 'prototype'. Some of the York foliage borders also have loose stylistic affinities with St Denis examples, and both York Minster and St Denis contained windows dedicated to the Life of St Benedict. The recent identification of a further fragment of the St Denis window at Raby Castle in County Durham (others are preserved at Twycross, Leicestershire) has demonstrated that the English and French windows had scenes in common, both being indebted to an eleventh-century illuminated manuscript life of the saint made for the Abbey of Monte Cassino, the Benedictine founder's house.

In the north ambulatory of St Denis are the remains of an extraordinary window filled with griffon medallions surrounded by rich foliage. The window has been heavily restored, but antiquarian evidence confirms the authenticity of the design. It is difficult to imagine Suger's contemporary and correspondent, St Bernard of Clairvaux, founder of the more austere Cistercian Order, approving of this opulence. In his *Apologia* of 1124 he criticized the use of luxurious materials and figurative imagery in monastic art and architecture, singling out in particular 'those ridiculous monsters' commonly used in the sculptural decoration of the cloister. His views were formalized in the Statutes of the Order, the earliest of which perhaps date

**Above** A mid twelfth-century grisaille design from Bonlieu, after Abbé Texier (1850). Obedient to the teachings of their founder St Bernard, many Cistercian abbeys in the twelfth century glazed their churches and cloisters with non-figural grisaille, developing a wide range of inventive patterns.

**Below** The enamel plaques completed in 1181 by the Mosan metalworker Nicholas of Verdun, achieve a remarkable sculptural plasticity and naturalism, the result in part of a familiarity with late antique art.

from 1151, which forbade the use of coloured and figurative glass in the windows of Cistercian churches. Thus, just as Suger's St Denis was receiving international acclamation for its magnificence, the Cistercians were adopting an aesthetic that gave impetus to the development of a wealth of non-figurative decoration in stained glass. These Cistercian 'grisaille' windows of vegetal or geometric patterns used little or no paint. Their decorative motifs were derived from sculpture and were to be used in glass, wall-painting, tiles and manuscript illumination. One of the earliest examples of this type of glazing to remain *in situ* is in the French Cistercian church of Obazine (Corrèze), datable to *c.*1175–90, while at Heiligenkreuz in Austria the cloister glazing of *c.*1200–25 would have received St Bernard's approval for its appropriately unprovocative foliage grisaille. This type of glazing was not confined to churches of the Cistercian Order. Grisaille windows were popular wherever taste or reasons of economy called for plainer glazing.

By far the largest quantity of surviving twelfth-century stained glass dates from the period *c.*1180–1200 and reveals a greater degree of stylistic diversity. In the last quarter of the twelfth century, artists in all media were experimenting with a more naturalistic and volumetric style, which drew on Byzantine art and, perhaps more importantly, on late classical models. In cities such as Reims, for example, substantial remains of the Roman past served as a reminder of the artistic achievements of the classical world. The third-century Porte de Mars survives to this day, and one of the most classically inspired pieces of early thirteenth-century sculpture, the Visitation group from the west façade of the Cathedral, is eloquent proof that craftsmen and artists were examining late classical art with excitement and interest.

One of the earliest and most important works in this 'transitional' style which spans the divide between Romanesque and Gothic, antedating the Reims sculptures by thirty to forty years, is the signed and dated series of *champlevé* enamel plaques made in 1181 for the ambo (or pulpit) of the Abbey of Klosterneuberg (near Vienna) by the Mosan artist Nicholas of Verdun. Nicholas emerges as one of the outstanding figures in a substantial line of metalworkers from the valley of the Meuse, who had long been receptive to the influence of classical antiquity. Stained glass in the east of France and in the valleys of the Meuse and Rhine had always been affected by stylistic developments in metalwork of the area. The debt to Mosan metalwork of the mid-twelfth-century glass at Châlons-sur-Marne, for example, has been recognized for some time.

Although the delineation of the naked human form in Nicholas' ambo plaques retains the linear, decorative quality of Romanesque painting, the draped figures have a solidity and plasticity which is wholly naturalistic. The vigorous postures of the bodies can be discerned through the fabric and display an understanding of the articulation of the human form. The draperies themselves have completely abandoned the artificial clinging 'dampfold' of the Romanesque and in the most lively compositions, like Samson and the Lion, for example, drapery is used to give a sense of movement. In the composition of some of the scenes, notably the

Harrowing of Hell, Nicholas has adapted a specific classical model, that of Hercules drawing Cerebrus out of the Underworld, transmitted to the West through Byzantine models.

Recent research on some of the most important surviving stained-glass schemes of the period has established that glass-painters too were in the vanguard of this transitional evolution. Professor Caviness' work on the glazing of Canterbury Cathedral has demonstrated that the so-called Methusaleh Master, responsible for the clerestory figures of Methusaleh, Adam, Jared, Enoch, Lamech and Noah and some of the typological scenes in the north aisle, is Nicholas of Verdun's close contemporary and artistic equal. Indeed, England was in the forefront of that study of the literary and philosophical heritage of the classical past often described as the Twelfth-Century Renaissance. One of the most important figures concerned with work on the rediscovered works of Aristotle and with an appreciation of the Latin classics was John of Salisbury (c.1120–80), friend and companion in exile of Archbishop Thomas à Becket. John's education was an international one; he had studied theology and philosophy in Chartres and logic in Paris, and in 1172 he became Bishop of Chartres. His own writings, particularly his letters, reveal his deep-seated humanism. The Roman past was less ingrained in England than in France, but John relates how on a visit to Rome in 1149–50 Henry of Blois, Bishop of Winchester, had purchased classical statuary which he transported back to England.

The power of the Methusaleh Master's work is not solely the result of the size of his figures. They have a classical monumentality about them. Methusaleh sits pensively stroking his beard, his elbow resting on his raised knee, as he stares directly out of the window at the observer below; Lamech swivels on his throne; and Enoch starts with surprise as a heavenly hand grasps him by the wrist. In the aisle-level scene of Christ leading the Gentiles from idolatry, pagan belief is personified by a nude, horned idol who stands on a column in a perceptible *contrapposto*. In both this figure and the half-naked Adam, Romanesque abstraction has been replaced by a tentative naturalism.

Travel in the twelfth century was not confined to churchmen and monarchs. A convincing case has been made for the attribution of the clerestory figures from St Remi in Reims, St Yved at Braine and those by the 'Petronella Master' at Canterbury to a single workshop. Although completed panels of stained glass were often transported considerable distances, it is extremely unlikely that the panels in Canterbury were merely exported from France. The career of the twelfth-century Cathedral's first architect, William of Sens, reveals that artists were mobile, following major commissions wherever they were to be found. Peter of Celle, Abbot of St Remi in Reims where the workshop is presumed to have been based, was a friend of John of Salisbury, who had spent part of his career in Canterbury. Family ties linked Queen Eleanor of Aquitaine and Agnes Dreux, the patroness of the St Yved glazing. This network of international relationships made the world of the late twelfth century far more close-knit than the physical distances and difficulties of travel might lead us to expect.

Apart from Reims, the city of Troyes in Champagne was also a significant

**Above** Like Nicholas of Verdun, the Methusaleh Master of Canterbury Cathedral drew upon ancient and Byzantine models for his brooding figure of Methusaleh (c.1175–80) made for the choir clerestory.

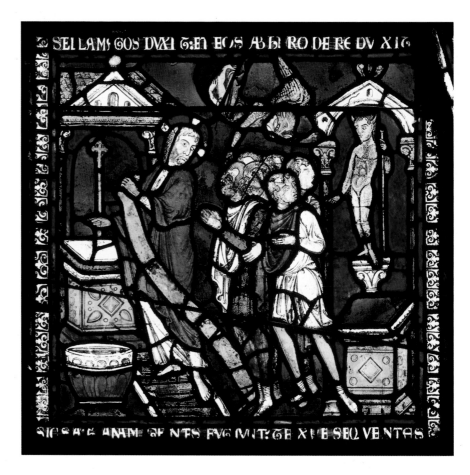

**Right** The allegorical scene of Christ leading the Gentiles from Pagan gods (*c.*1180) in the Canterbury choir aisle includes a tiny blue idol in classical *contrapposto* stance, perhaps copied from a piece of late antique sculpture.

glass-painting centre. A series of panels which may have been made for the parish church of St Etienne *c.*1190–1200 are now dispersed in a number of museum collections on both sides of the Atlantic (the Victoria and Albert Museum in London, the Metropolitan Museum of Art in New York, the Glencairn Museum, Bryn Athyn, Pennsylvania, and Wellesley College Museum in Massachusetts) and can be linked by their distinctive painting style. The figures are rounded, solid, and in the painterly modelling of their faces follow exactly the tonal painting techniques advocated by Theophilus. In their meticulous attention to detail they resemble the work of manuscript illuminators and it has been suggested that their creator worked in both media.

Although the Empire of the Caesars had ceased to exist, medieval Europe still possessed an emperor, for on Christmas Day 800 Pope Hadrian had crowned Charlemagne, and his Hohenstauffen successors continued to wear the crown of the Holy Roman Empire. Cities with imperial connections (Aachen, Trier, Regensburg and Strasbourg, for example) looked to the classical imperial past with particular interest. Strasbourg was situated near the Hohenstauffen castle of Hagenau and had been founded by the Emperor Otto in the tenth century. Among the surviving Romanesque panels preserved from the building replaced by the present Gothic church, are the remains of a series of life-size figures of emperors in appropriate regalia. They were given great prominence in the Ottonian Cathedral and probably stood in the north windows of the nave. Compared to the Reims and Canterbury clerestory figures, the slightly later

Strasbourg emperors appear rather flat and their banded patterned robes and austere frontal poses are reminiscent of the Ausburg prophets created a century earlier. One of the best-preserved and most impressive figures is that of a seated, nimbused emperor, perhaps representing Charlemagne, now in the Musée de l'Oeuvre Notre Dame. His prominent eyes are separate leaded inserts, which give him an intense and compelling stare. His brooding presence personifies the emperor's right, albeit rarely exercised, to occupy a place in the western gallery of imperial foundations.

Remaining in the Cathedral are the paired figures of St John the Evangelist and St John the Baptist, located in the east wall of the north transept. These figures reveal the potent influence of Byzantine art which is such an important characteristic of the twelfth-century Strasbourg glass. The distinctive poses, arched niches and inscribed scrolls are all derived from Byzantine models, which were particularly important to artists in eastern France and Germany. The monumental mosaics of Sicily, part of the Hohenstauffen inheritance, served as a conduit for these influences. The Archbishop of Strasbourg was a supporter of the Emperor Frederick Barbarossa, whose power-base was in Sicily.

The poses of the two St Johns as well as the Byzantine 'Theotokos' pose of the enthroned Virgin Mary from the Jesse Tree and the Coronation panel were not confined to stained glass. They were paralleled in the manuscript *Hortus Deliciarum* (*The Garden of Delight*), created in Alsace by Harrade of Landsberg between *c.*1176 and 1196. The original manuscript was destroyed in a fire in 1870 but is known from tracings made earlier in

**Above** This imposing figure of an emperor (*c.*1200) may have been made for the western tribune gallery of the now destroyed Romanesque cathedral in Strasbourg. It is now in the Musée de l'Oeuvre Notre Dame.

**Left** A number of museum collections contain distinctive panels originating from five separate windows, dating from *c.*1180, thought to have come from either Troyes Cathedral or a parish church in the city. This panel, now in the Victoria and Albert Museum in London, depicts one of the Temptations of Christ.

the nineteenth century. Indeed, the drapery style of the earlier of the Strasbourg figures is reminiscent of the style of the *Hortus*.

Far closer to the sculptural plasticity of the works of Nicholas of Verdun are the surviving figures of a Jesse Tree from the Romanesque choir of the Cathedral of Freiburg im Breisgau, begun in 1200. For their relatively small size, these nine figures are remarkably monumental. Each one is enclosed in a medallion, once arranged in a series of vertical rows, with Christ's ancestors in the centre and the prophets at the sides. This German design differed considerably from the St Denis type, which shows the seated figures grasping the stems of the vine in which they perch. Each of the Freiburg figures is labelled and also carries an appropriate attribute, another most unusual feature of this window.

Elsewhere in Germany the 'damp-fold' Romanesque drapery style was remarkably persistent. This is exemplified by the miniatures in the sumptuous Missal commissioned *c*.1215 by Abbot Berthold of Weingarten (Swabia), in which draperies covering the ample figures are modelled with surface colour, while faces have an anxious, almost agonized intensity. This painting style is paralleled in a somewhat softer and calmer form in glass by the impressive remains of a Jesse Tree of *c*.1230 in Regensburg Cathedral. The figures in the central narrative medallions have a solidity and a grave, monumental solemnity that belies their fluttering draperies. The decorative qualities of Romanesque art were only reluctantly eschewed in Germany and existed alongside the lively, small-scale elegance of Gothic painting well into the thirteenth century.

**Above**  The splendid Missal of *c*.1215, one of a number of books commissioned by Abbot Berthold of Weingarten, persists in the use of Romanesque 'damp fold' drapery.

**Right**  The Regensburg Cathedral Jesse Tree (*c*.1230), combines scenes from the Infancy of Christ with a genealogical tree in an inventive variation on the theme.

**Opposite**  Freiburg Cathedral, begun in 1200, preserves nine medallions from an extremely unusual Jesse Tree, probably completed before 1218. The medallions contain both labels and attributes for each figure and have reduced the Tree to foliage sprays.

# THE GREAT CATHEDRAL AGE

By the year 1200 France had emerged as the most powerful country in northern Europe. Under the rule of King Philip I (Philip Augustus), the Crown had extended its rule over almost all of what is now modern France, and the death of King Richard I of England opened the way for the conquest of Normandy and Anjou in the west. In the south the campaign against the Cathar heretics (the Albigensian Crusade) re-established royal influence in an area that had shrugged it off for centuries. The prestige of the monarchy was further enhanced by Philip's saintly crusader successor Louis IX (1226–70), Saint Louis, for whom the glorious Sainte-Chapelle was built. French political influence was matched by growing cultural and artistic influence. It was in this century of French political pre-eminence, that the Gothic style, first developed in northern France and already having an impact in England, came to be widely copied, penetrating the countries of the Holy Roman Empire and Italy.

Early Gothic churches, such as Notre-Dame in Paris, Laon and Canterbury Cathedrals, had far larger windows than their Romanesque predecessors. They are often difficult to see from the ground, however, being set deeply into the thickness of their walls, or obscured in the recesses of their galleries. At Chartres Cathedral, rebuilt after a fire in 1194 that destroyed all but its Romanesque west front, the architect created a thin, flat interior elevation, in which the glazed lower and upper stories are of equal size and are clearly visible from the ground, whether the viewer stands directly in front of them or looks diagonally across the church. From c.1230, the triforium, the gallery running between the high clerestory windows above

**Above**   The rose window of Lausanne Cathedral, made by Pierre d'Arras, active in the city 1217–35, depicts a complex medieval image of the universe, reflecting the scholarly theological tastes of its donor, Bishop Boniface of Brussels. Here we see a detail of Luna, the Moon.

**Opposite**   The south transept rose of Chartres Cathedral was given c.1221–30 by members of the Dreux-Bretagne family, who appear with their heraldry at the base of the window.

and the aisles below, also began to be pierced and glazed, adding yet another zone of glazing requiring the glass-painter's attention. The architectural formula exemplified by Chartres afforded far greater prominence to the role of stained glass in the decoration of the interior, and it is therefore fitting that Chartres preserves such a wealth of thirteenth-century stained glass, offering a glimpse of the medieval vision of what a great Gothic interior should look like.

The increase in window size made possible by the lightening of the vaults and the development of more complex methods of buttressing, demanded a new approach to the design of figurative windows. The majority of Romanesque windows contain relatively few figures, conceived on a large scale and superimposed in a small number of horizontal tiers, while the lateral spread of scenes and figures is relatively limited. The wider and taller Gothic window openings required a different layout. The window itself was commonly divided into numerous compartments, often displaying a wide variety of geometric shapes. The metal armatures spanning the window and onto which the individual panels were fixed, were bent into complex shapes to accommodate the glaziers' ingenuity, a task entrusted to skilled smiths and metalworkers, with whom the glaziers must have worked closely in creating their window designs. During the first half of the thirteenth century a comparatively small amount of light-coloured glass was employed, making the windows appear far darker than their Romanesque predecessors. The spaces in between the figurative panels were filled with richly coloured decorative motifs, often derived from foliage forms interpreted in a formalized manner. Every piece of glass was painted; all the lozenges, squares, leaves and palmettes in the backgrounds were highly painted and every narrative compartment had a painted fillet around it. This presented the glass-painting workshops with an enormous amount of intricate cutting, painting, firing and leading. There is evidence, not surprisingly, that as a result of this pressure, glass-painters streamlined their painting techniques. The elaborate three-tonal procedure described by Theophilus gave way to a greater reliance on basic trace-lines and a simple wash, although even the wash was sometimes omitted. In some respects, this loosening-up of the technical procedures led to a greater naturalism in painting, although there is also a perceptible loss in legibility.

The thirteenth-century window became an important vehicle for story-telling, and in northern Europe stained glass emerged as the most important

**Left** The heads in this panel depicting the Marriage at Cana, made for the Infancy of Christ window in Rouen Cathedral *c.*1230, are painted in the simplified and economical techniques of the thirteenth century. The panel is now in the church of St Mary and St Nicholas in Wilton (Wiltshire).

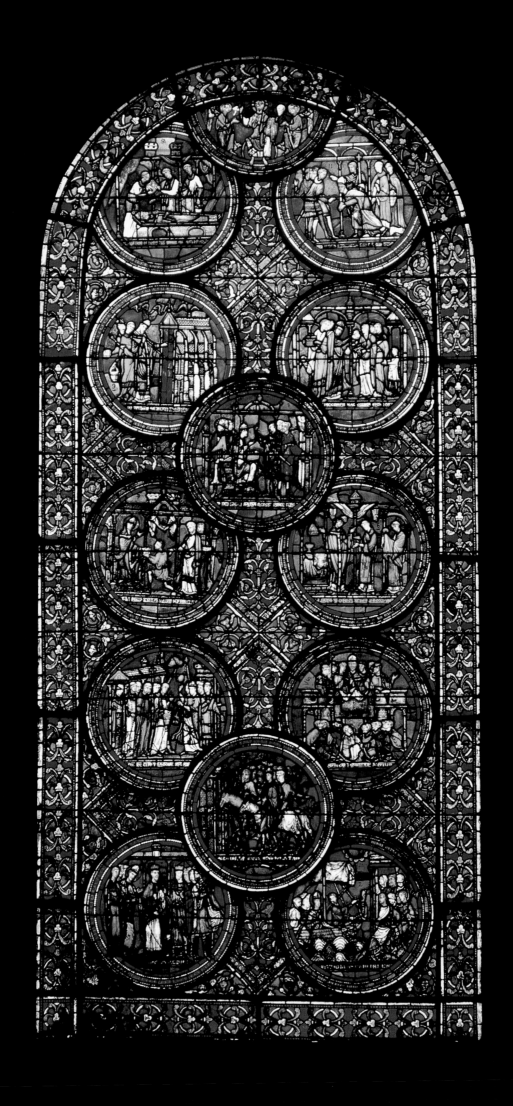

form of monumental painting. This development had begun in the last quarter of the twelfth century. The typological Bible windows of c.1180 in the north choir aisle of Canterbury Cathedral already contained superimposed tiers of figurative panels, interspersed with rich foliage panels. The enormous size of many thirteenth-century windows, which were often placed at great height, combined with their more numerous and intricate arrangements of compartments, provided considerable narrative opportunity but frequently make the windows rather difficult to decipher. The Life of St Thomas à Becket in Chartres Cathedral, for example, unfolds in twenty-two individual scenes, with an additional three panels depicting the activities of the tanners, who donated the window. In the vertiginous windows of the upper chapel of the Sainte-Chapelle, the story of Esther requires 129 separate narrative scenes and each window contains well over two hundred compartments. The story was usually intended to be read from the bottom to the top, allowing the martyrdom and apotheosis of a saint to appear as the spiritual and literal culmination of a window. The use of radiating, lobed divisions could, however, introduce an element of confusion in an age in which the concept of clockwise would have had little relevance. Scenes were generally positioned so as to be read from left to right, although a desire for symmetry and the inclination to place the most important scene or individual figure in the centre of the window would sometime interrupt this arrangment.

In the rose window, representing for many people the apogee of the Gothic stained-glass window, the designer was faced with a particularly challenging task. This form evolved quickly in the thirteenth century, becoming ever larger in size and more complex in the patterns of its tracery. The position of the rose window, typically in the west façade or the terminal wall of a transept, made it particularly suitable for a pictorial account of the great themes of Christian history – the Creation, the Last Judgment, Christ in Glory or the Coronation of the Virgin Mary. The great rose window in the south transept wall at Lausanne contains one of the most ambitious schemes of all, a complex picture of the cosmological universe as understood in the Middle Ages.

The Biblical narrative remained the basic iconographical source for stained glass. In the Bible itself, Christ had described Jonah's deliverance from the belly of the whale as a symbol of his own Resurrection, and St Paul compared the Crossing of the Red Sea to Baptism. This concept of 'type' and 'antitype', in which principal events in the New Testament were shown to have been prefigured by events in the Old, became extremely popular with early Christian theologians, particularly those in Alexandria, who were able to find typological parallels for almost every Biblical event. Typological interpretation dates back a long way, and by the thirteenth century it was an established way of representing Biblical history. Chartres, Le Mans, Tours, Bourges, all had thirteenth-century typological windows. By 1200 Canterbury Cathedral already had twelve such windows and they probably also featured in the thirteenth-century glazing scheme at Lincoln. A large number of typological *Bibelfenster* (Bible windows) survive in Germany, in Cologne Cathedral (from the Dominican church), in the Franciscan church

**Opposite**  The Life of St Thomas à Becket unfolds in thirteen clustered medallions in this window in Sens Cathedral, made in the first quarter of the thirteenth century. The heavy, dark lines separating the compartments are the metal armatures supporting the panels in the window opening.

**Above**   Moses receives the tablets of the law in this window of *c.*1280, made for a *Bibelfenster* in the Dominican church in Cologne. Its topological partner is the Pentecost. The church was destroyed in 1804 and its glass is now located in Cologne Cathedral.

**Above right**   This Old Testament scene of the Israelites crossing the Red Sea (*c.*1230) in Lincoln Cathedral would once have been paired with the Baptism of Christ from the New Testament, the event it prefigured.

at Esslingen, at Mönchengladbach and in the Dominican church at Wimpfen am Berg, and their popularity extended well into the fourteenth century. While typological scenes were interpreted in many artistic media, in the bas-reliefs on the west front of Amiens Cathedral, for example, in many respects stained glass was the most perfect vehicle for this type of complex juxtaposition of events. Catherine Brisac has very plausibly suggested that in the divisions of their pages and in their use of gold-leaf for their backgrounds the illuminators of the French thirteenth-century *Bibles Moralisées* (Moralized Bibles) were emulating stained-glass windows.

Another fruitful source for the glass-painter to draw upon was the wealth of apocryphal literature embellishing and expanding upon the Biblical narrative, and accepted as authentic throughout the Middle Ages. In particular, the enormous devotion to the Virgin Mary was not satisfied by the relatively meagre information supplied in the Gospels and the apocryphal texts were especially valuable in furnishing the details of her life that were eagerly sought by the faithful. These apocryphal texts, expressing the pious desire to know more of the sacred history than the New Testament provided, enormously enriched the visual fund that medieval artists could call upon. Of particular importance were the *Gospel of Pseudo-Matthew*, with its fund of stories about the infant Christ and his mother, the

*Protevangelium of James*, with its stories of the parentage, upbringing and education of the Virgin, and the *Gospel of Nicodemus*, devoted to the Passion of Christ and containing the account of his descent into Limbo and the Harrowing of Hell. Further details of Christ's Infancy and Passion were culled from *The Golden Legend* compiled in the mid thirteenth century by the Dominican Archbishop of Genoa, Jacob of Voragine.

*The Golden Legend*, with its wealth of anecdotal incident, was particularly valuable to artists as a manual on the lives of the saints. While individual histories existed for the many saints revered in the Middle Ages (two Lives of St Thomas à Becket, martyred in 1170, were written by Canterbury monks in the years immediately after his death, for example), in *The Golden Legend* the essential 'facts' were brought together in a single encyclopedic text. Secular literature was rarely the source of subject matter for stained glass, but could, on occasion, provide inspiration – the great Charlemagne window at Chartres, for example, is a faithful illustration of the epic poem *La Chanson de Roland*.

The thirteenth century also witnessed the increasing popularity of grisaille glass. Grisaille was particularly favoured by the Cistercian Order, obedient to the austere injunctions of St Bernard. One of the best preserved

**Below** The Charlemagne window (*c.*1220–25) in the choir of Chartres Cathedral depicts the epic events related in the *Chanson de Roland*. In the many scenes in which the canonized king appears, his name, CAROLUS, identifies his figure.

**Above** The cloister of the Abbey of
Heiligenkreuz in Austria preserves the
largest surviving collection of Cistercian
grisaille. Ten bays contain over eighty
panels, glazed between c.1200 and c.1250.
The fleshy palmettes are painted on a
greenish tinted clear glass.

**Right** The north wall of the north
transept of York Minster is filled with mid
thirteenth-century grisaille, in a window
now known as the Five Sisters.

examples of Cistercian grisaille glazing can be found at Heiligenkreuz, near
Vienna. The scheme, dating from about 1220, occupies ten bays of the
cloister, that part of the monastery used for contemplation. The highly
complex formalized leaf forms rely on an intricate pattern of lead, skilfully
integrated into the design and reinforced by a great deal of painted detail,
particularly in the cross-hatched backgrounds. Grisaille windows were by
no means confined to the Cistercians, however, and were popular in the
glazing of cathedral chapter houses, cloisters and other contexts demanding
a higher degree of illumination. Salisbury Cathedral contained a large
number of grisaille windows, painted and unpainted, both in the church and
in the chapter house. One of the most spectacular uses of grisaille is found in
the north transept of York Minster, where the lancets filling the north wall,
known as the Five Sisters, are filled entirely with painted grisaille. The
complex cut-line and extensive painting involved in the creation of many of
these grisaille windows means that despite their reliance on white glass
(coloured glass is used very sparingly), they were often labour- and

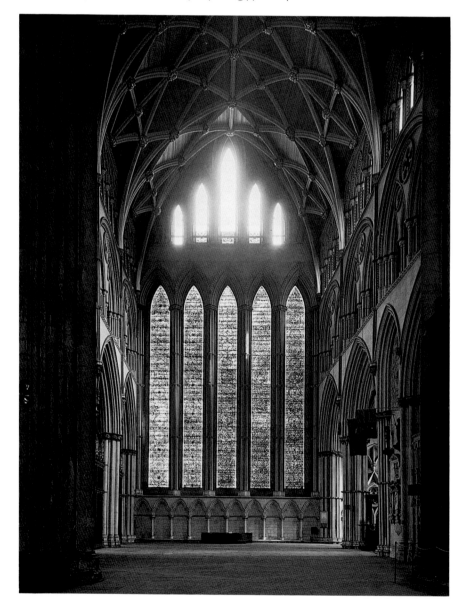

**Left**    Both Chartres and Bourges Cathedrals have windows dedicated to the parable of the Good Samaritan. The Chartres window, seen here, is designed to be read from top to bottom, left to right.

skill-intensive and so cannot be regarded simply as a cheap alternative to coloured windows; an aesthetic consideration must also be taken into account. In less prominent positions, entirely unpainted grisaille was used, as in the clerestory windows at Salisbury and in the church of the Valeria at Sitten in Switzerland, and even here, the panels have a decorative quality in addition to a practical function.

Chartres remains one of the most seductive of all medieval cathedrals, and its stained glass has cast a spell on the imagination of generations of visitors. The Cathedral preserves the most extensive collection of medieval windows anywhere in the world: 165 windows and three glazed roses contain medieval glass. The whole ensemble was created in a remarkably short space of time. Construction of the Gothic church began in 1194 and by 1220 had progressed sufficiently for altars to be set up there. The earliest windows are those in the nave dating from between c.1200 and 1210–15. The latest windows to be completed, those of the choir and the eastern face of the north transept, date from c.1235, meaning that the whole scheme took barely thirty-five years to complete. The lower windows contain numerous intricate compartments filled with lively scenes and figures, while the upper windows generally contain one single large

**Above** The Chartres windows offer numerous glimpses of the commercial life of a prosperous market city. The fur merchants and drapers shown in this detail were the joint donors of the St James window.

figure per bay. Some attempt was made to impose a coherent iconographic plan on the whole: the upper windows of the apse, for example, are devoted to the Glorification of the Virgin Mary, to whom the church is dedicated, and whose reliquary had miraculously survived the fire of 1194. The western wall of the nave was devoted to the Life and Passion of Christ, with the Last Judgment in the rose above. The original intention may have been to fill the northern aisle windows with stories from the Old Testament, and windows on the south with stories from the New. The subjects of other windows were determined by their proximity to a particular altar. This rationale was soon to be swept aside by the tastes and preferences of the donors who gave the individual windows, and it was the Cathedral's success in attracting secular patronage that ensured the completion of the scheme in record time.

A large number of glaziers was involved, and the importance of Chartres in stained-glass history lies not just in the quantity of its glass, but in its significance for the formation of glazing workshops throughout northern France in the first half of the thirteenth century. Such a prestigious scheme attracted artists from a large area – the influence of Bourges and Sens has been detected – and once at work in the city, the glass-painters were to influence each other and to carry what they had experienced on to other major sites. Detailed stylistic analysis of the Chartres workshops is only just beginning, but it is already clear that one glass-painter was responsible for the repair of the twelfth-century glass in the west wall, while another group of artists produced the St Leobinus, St Nicholas and Noah windows, with a third workshop responsible for the Death of the Virgin Mary, the Mary Magdalene and Typological Passion. The St Eustace, the Good Samaritan and Joseph windows all display different characteristics. In the choir, where the most elaborate windows are to be found, at least two more workshops were active, one responsible for the splendid Charlemagne window (given by the furriers) and the other for the St James window. These two workshops produced between them some of the most effective story-telling windows in the cathedral, uncluttered, legible and harmonious.

The early thirteenth-century windows at Canterbury Cathedral have a similar quality. The windows of the Trinity Chapel, the backdrop of St Thomas à Becket's sumptuous shrine, were glazed in the period c.1200–20,

**Left**   The cure of Mathilda, a madwoman from Cologne (c.1220), is one of St Thomas à Becket's many miracles depicted in the choir ambulatory of Canterbury Cathedral. Gesture plays an important part in the narration of the stories.

**Above**  Hezekiah, a figure from the genealogical series from the eastern clerestory in Canterbury Cathedral, is painted in a refined, small-scale style in marked contrast to the monumentality of the earlier Methusaleh from the same series (see p. 47).

**Right**  The luminous atmosphere pervading the upper chapel of the Sainte-Chapelle is created by the stained glass in its tall thin windows. The scheme glorifies the Passion of Christ, relics of which were preserved in the chapel.

although the project was interrupted by the Interdict and the exile of the Canterbury monks between 1207 and 1213. It is thought that the scheme had been completed by the time Becket's remains were translated from his tomb in the crypt to the new shrine in the centre of the Trinity Chapel on 7 July 1220. In contrast to the solemn and stately figures of the choir clerestory, the Becket Miracle windows in the ambulatory have a small-scale liveliness emphasized by the fluttering draperies. This reduction of scale is also apparent in the few surviving clerestory windows made for the Trinity Chapel. Compared to the windows made in the period c.1180–1200, the windows of the Gothic phase have been streamlined. The decorative elements and the backgrounds are no longer as elaborate and highly detailed. This in no way detracts from the legibility of the scenes, however. Gestures lend the scenes a clarity and vigour, enhanced by the silhouetting of the figures against their rich blue blackgrounds. During the Interdict, some of the Canterbury glaziers probably shared the monks' exile in France, which would explain the affinities between the Canterbury glass and windows of the same date at Bourges and Sens.

In the second quarter of the thirteenth century, Paris re-established its artistic and cultural pre-eminence. This was fostered by the personal

interest in the arts displayed by King Louis IX. His reputation for piety and wisdom was an important factor in popularizing the artistic styles associated with his court. A new 'court style' in architecture emerged, termed 'Rayonnant' because of the radiating patterns of the rose windows that play such an important part in this style. Not only did windows become larger and more numerous, but the tracery filling them became more complex and delicate, and tracery patterns began to be applied to bare areas of wall to create a more decorative and textured surface effect. One of the earliest examples of this new style was the transept and nave of St Denis, although none of the stained glass from this part of the church has survived. The most striking example, and the one most significant for its stained glass, is the Sainte-Chapelle in Paris.

This exquisite chapel, built to house the relics of Christ's Passion, purchased from the Byzantine Emperor Baldwin II in 1239, resembles a jewelled reliquary casket. Work began in 1240 or 1242 and the immense glazing scheme, of which only the upper chapel remains, was executed between 1242 and 1248. Despite its imperfect state, it is the stained glass which transforms this small chapel into a masterpiece. The western rose was renewed in the late fifteenth century and the thirteenth-century glass has suffered considerable damage and extensive restoration. Nonetheless, the interior of the upper chapel continues to offer one of the most impressive displays of medieval stained glass. The iconographic scheme was ambitious, portraying the history of the Universe, from the Creation to the end of time. The axial window was devoted to Christ's Passion. Three distinct groups of glass-painters have been identified, supervised by a single master who ensured the coherence of the scheme. In order to cope with the considerable demands placed upon them, the glaziers simplified the framing of their scenes, repeating the armature shapes and favouring the half-medallion in particular. The background mosaics were almost mass-produced. The style of the figure-drawing has also undergone a change. Symmetrical compositions were favoured and the drawing became harder and more angular. Figures have a calm, unflurried quality, even in the scenes of violence and movement.

Traces of this change can already be detected in the earlier St Chéron window at Chartres and are also found in the other great Parisian glazing scheme of the period, now dispersed between a number of museum colletions, that of the destroyed Lady Chapel and Refectory of St Germain-des-Prés. This glass, executed between 1234 (or 1235) and 1243 (or 1244) displays a similarly 'hardened' style of painting, which is found in a fully matured form in the Sainte-Chapelle.

The craftsmen of the Sainte-Chapelle workshops were exceptionally skilled technicians. As appropriate when working for the king, they were using glass of the highest quality and the panels display remarkably little corrosion. The painted detail is also well preserved. Not surprisingly, the services of the artists of the Sainte-Chapelle were sought elsewhere. They have been identified at work in the nave at Soissons Cathedral and were also involved in the transept glazing at Notre-Dame in Paris.

England, with so little surviving thirteenth-century glass, was the European

**Above** The parish church at Twycross in Leicestershire, England preserves six panels from the Sainte-Chapelle (1244–8). The Deposition from the Cross is excellently preserved; a modern copy replaces it in the Passion window in the Sainte-Chapelle itself. It perfectly illustrates the simple but effective painting styles adopted by Parisian workshops in the mid-thirteenth century.

**Above** Although the architecture of the western choir of Naumberg Cathedral (begun *c*.1250) employs northern French Gothic formulas, the stained glass in its windows remains faithful to the distinctive, jagged *Zackenstil* (broken fold style), giving the figures of apostle and saints a lively, restless feel.

country most receptive to French ideas of Gothic, although English artists and architects quickly evolved their own Gothic formulas. At Westminster Abbey, Henry III built the English response to Rayonnant, a building absorbing many French features, but with English ingredients added. The chapter house, begun in 1246, is a typical English octagonal structure, but in its use of large, refined traceried windows, it is the closest Westminster gets to the 'cage of glass' idea expressed in the Sainte-Chapelle. Nothing survives of its original thirteenth-century glazing, although it is clear from the vestiges remaining elsewhere in the Abbey that Henry's church was richly glazed. At Salisbury, where the Westminster model was extremely influential, the original chapter house glazing survived until the nineteenth century and combined a small number of figures, a display of heraldry and large areas of elaborate foliage grisaille, creating a bright, silvery effect, preserved today in the careful nineteenth-century copies of the badly damaged medieval originals. The mixing of rich colour and light grisaille was to become increasingly prevalent in the second half of the thirteenth century.

The picture in the countries of the Holy Roman Empire was rather different. As we have seen in the previous chapter, the Romanesque style was remarkably persistent and resilient. Its vitality is demonstrated by the evolution, *c*.1240–50, of a distinctive style defined in connection with the glass of St Elizabeth's church in Marburg as *Zackenstil* or 'broken fold style', named for its jagged, angular treatment of drapery. Its origins lie in the northern parts of the Empire, in Thuringia and Saxony, where it is found in many forms of monumental painting. One of the most pronounced versions is in the Trinity Altarpiece made for Soest, *c*.1230–40, now in the Staatliche Gemäldegalerie in Berlin. In stained glass one of the most remarkable examples is to be found in the windows of *c*.1250 in the western choir of Naumberg, where the glass-painters were no doubt responding to the stimulus of the extraordinary sculpture in the choir. When it comes to the dissemination of French ideas of Gothic, two monuments are of the greatest importance – Strasbourg and Cologne Cathedrals. The glazing of the nave at Strasbourg, built between *c*.1254 and *c*.1275, was taking place against a background of Parisian influence. The nave itself expresses Parisian architectural ideas. The choir screen (*c*.1260) was probably the work of a Reims workshop. By *c*.1265 the Strasbourg workshops had completed their work on the triforium and clerestory and dispersed to work further east, taking their familiarity with French ideas with them, as far afield as Brandenburg Cathedral and Wiener Neustadt. Cologne Cathedral, begun in 1248, was modelled on Amiens and was the most French of the German cathedrals, although in stained glass Gothic formulas were relatively slow to penetrate. Fully fledged Gothic figures are only found in the first quarter of the fourteenth century. German workshops proved themselves to be exceptionally inventive in the creation of new picture cycles, particularly in the service of the Francisan Order. This ingenuity is demonstrated in the glass of the church of St Elizabeth in Marburg. St Elizabeth (1207–31), the widow of Louis IV, Margrave of Thuringia, became a Franciscan tertiary after her husband's death and devoted her life to acts of humility and charity, living out her days in Marburg. She was canonized in 1235, the year in which the western choir of the church dedicated to her was begun. The eleven scenes (originally twelve) devoted to her life, so fresh in the memory of those commissioning the windows, were conceived in terms of the acts of mercy commended by Christ in St Matthew's Gospel. In another window she is shown in glory with St Francis and the Virgin and Child. The Franciscan church, the Barfüsserkirche, in Erfurt, was begun barely two years after the death of Francis in 1226. He was canonized in 1228 and the Erfurt windows preserve two scenes from a window of c.1235–45 depicting his life, including his receipt of the stigmata in 1224. Together with the Marburg panels, these are the earliest examples of Franciscan iconography north of the Alps. It is not surprising, therefore, that in seeking assistance with the glazing of the upper church at Assisi, the Franciscans looked to Germany.

The history of stained glass in Italy gains momentum in the thirteenth century. Although some of the very earliest painted glass yet discovered, possibly of sixth century date, has been found in Italy, very little survives from the intervening period; two panels of c.1200 preserved in the treasury of Aosta Cathedral cannot be described as Gothic and are of a provincial style and quality. At Assisi, in the basilica constructed on the site of St Francis's death, stained glass is an important, integral part of the decoration. The basilica was begun in 1228, the year in which Francis was canonized,

**Left**  The Barfüsserkirche (Franciscan church) in Erfurt was rebuilt at the beginning of the fourteenth century, but this panel of 1235–45 was preserved, with two others, from the earlier church, no doubt because of its special subject matter. St Francis had received the stigmata in September 1224, making this one of the earliest representations of the miracle in Franciscan art.

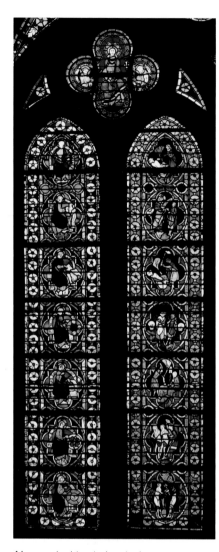

**Above** In this window in the upper basilica of San Francesco, Assisi, the story of the Creation (left-hand light) and the early stories from the book of Genesis (right-hand light) are depicted in one of those windows attributed to a German master glass-painter active c.1240–60.

**Opposite** The rose window in the apse of Siena Cathedral has frequently been attributed on stylistic grounds to the hand of the great painter Duccio. While his influence can certainly be detected, the framing around the saints is reminiscent of German windows (see p. 66).

and was consecrated by Pope Innocent IV in 1253, although the glass probably dates from the period 1240 to 1260. The windows depict a typological cycle of the Life of Christ, including a series of his appearances after the Resurrection, and is unequalled in its iconographic complexity, some scenes as yet defying identification. This reflects the prestige of this church, the holiest place of the Franciscan Order. The glaziers responsible seem to have been German, and links with the glazing workshops of Erfurt have been suggested. Two groups of glass-painters have been identified, and in the work of the second, associated with the 'Master of St Francis', the vigorous plasticity of the figures and the introduction of a spatial dimension show that Italian stained glass was already participating in the pictorial revolution in which Italy led the way.

The remarkable rose window in Siena Cathedral (datable to the period 1287–8 on documentary evidence) continues to use Germanic motifs, such as the 'keyhole' frames around the outer figures, but in the perspectival articulation of the throne on which Christ and the Virgin are seated and the desks at which the Evangelists write, the glass-painters already show a considerable mastery of spatial effects. The window, made for the former apse, has been attributed by some writers to Duccio and his stylistic influence is very clearly felt.

By 1260 stained glass in France was entering a new phase. Panels of silvery grisaille, already used extensively in those areas requiring a higher degree of illumination, now began to be combined with coloured figurative panels. Existing alongside this new type of window were a series of windows faithful to the older formulas. Almost nothing survives in Paris from the period 1260–1300, but survivals in the Île-de-France demonstrate that the seeds sewn by the Sainte-Chapelle had borne fruit. The miniaturist work found in Parisian manuscripts of the same period can be seen echoed in glass at St Sulpice-de-Favières. The church preserves two windows of c.1260, and a Nativity and an Adoration of the Magi of 1280. In the earlier glass the full-colour medallion formula typical of the Sainte-Chapelle is employed, but the number of figures in each panel has been drastically reduced, giving greater clarity to the scenes; illegibility was clearly recognized to be at risk in the 'full-colour' window. In the later glass, the medallion frame has been replaced by a simple canopy and the drapery has become softer and freer in its folds.

Colour-saturated backgrounds continued to be used by the glaziers working at Holy Trinity in Fécamp in Normandy. The Saint Catherine and Saint Margaret windows of c.1275 are filled with cusped quatrefoil frames, set into rich trellis backgrounds. The tiny, doll-like figures stand in swaying, sinuous poses which anticipate some of the stylistic characteristics of early fourteenth-century stained glass, while retaining so many elements derived from an earlier tradition. By this date, glaziers working at Tours Cathedral had already designed a new type of window, perfectly suited to the Gothic traceried window, with its tall thin lights divided by mullions. After a period of experimentation, considered in the next chapter, it was this figure-and-canopy formula that was to emerge as the characteristic window type of the fourteenth and fifteenth centuries.

# THE SILVER STAIN REVOLUTION

A comparison of one of the legendary windows of the Sainte-Chapelle in Paris of c.1248 with the Annunciation window in the clerestory of St Ouen at Rouen of c.1325 demonstrates the veracity of Emile Male's observation that 'nothing resembles a thirteenth-century window less than a fourteenth-century one'. Design, figure style, palette and sentiment have all undergone a dramatic change. And yet many of the compositional and colouristic changes that characterize stained glass of the fourteenth century can already be traced in the stained glass of the last quarter of the thirteenth century, demonstrating the artificiality of dividing history too inflexibly into centuries.

Nonetheless, the St Ouen Annunciation represents a remarkable departure from the densely packed 'full-colour' effect of the thirteenth century. The Rouen figures are slender, tall, almost elongated, and sinuous. They stand alone in the compartment of a single light and gesture to each other across the physical divide of the window mullion. Their figures are framed not by geometrical shapes, but by pinnacled canopies that accurately emulate the architectural forms in the window opening they occupy, forms which are found increasingly frequently applied in decorative ways to the plain masonry of the church interior. The figures are no longer divided from one another by panels of lush and colourful foliage, but by zones of silvery white glass. White glass is also used far more prominently in the figurative panels themselves. The foliage decorating the zones of white glass is no longer formalized and stiff, but trails with naturalistic exuberance, like tendrils climbing through a trellis. Lively foliage is also found in the borders of the windows. The range of colours used is wide. The thirteenth-century

**Above** The choir clerestory windows in Cologne Cathedral, executed in the first quarter of the fourteenth century, have adopted most of the stylistic formulas of French Gothic, although the light grisaille glass is concentrated in the upper parts of the window, throwing light onto the vault above.

**Below** Elegance personified in the Annunciation to the Virgin in the church of St Ouen in Rouen. This glass, dating from c.1325, exemplifies the refinement of Parisian styles of the first quarter of the fourteenth century, although little glass now survives in the capital.

palette in which red and blue are conspicuous gives way to one with a prominent range of earthy colours and a bright leafy green, a particular favourite of English glass-painters.

Stained glass of the fourteenth century is a truly architectural medium, for it is no longer the metal glazing armatures that supply coherence to the window, but the structure of the stained glass itself in the form of the architectural canopies that frame the figures and scenes. The canopies occupy at least as much space as the figures, and their verticality carries the eye upwards. Thus the stained glass enhances the effect of slender verticality sought by the architect, and in the plethora of pinnacles, buttresses, crockets and gables, the vocabulary of the mason is perfectly echoed by the repertoire of the glass-painter. In the course of the fourteenth century, the canopies in stained glass became increasingly complex, pierced with niches and aedicules sometimes filled with figures. The St Ouen canopies contain tiers of figures dressed in costumes characteristic of different social orders. In the Lady Chapel glazing in Ely Cathedral, the canopies of c.1340–9 are peopled by knights and peasants. The 'figure and canopy' formula emerged as a response to the widespread adoption of elaborate stone window tracery, widely popularized in the second half of the thirteenth century.

Plate tracery, a pierced stone frame which divides the window opening into compartments beneath a simple oculus, appeared at Chartres c.1194–1220. Decorative traceries developed quickly, at Reims, Amiens and Soissons, becoming increasingly delicate and complex. The two main openings beneath an oculus at Chartres became four lights beneath a rose with subsidiary quatrefoils in the nave of Amiens, begun c.1220. By the second half of the thirteenth century structures like Sainte-Chapelle in Paris and St Urbain in Troyes had demonstrated how the solid wall mass could be dissolved to leave a cage of glass. In the early fourteenth century, particularly in England, window tracery became one of the most fertile areas of architectural decorative invention. The glass-painter's work was now accorded unprecedented prominence in the decoration of the wall and the glass-painter was asked to fill a slenderly proportioned tracery of pronounced verticality. The St Ouen window demonstrates how successfully the craftsman-designer met the challenge, although it is perhaps surprising that glaziers took quite so long to develop a response to this new window type.

Evidence of experimentation in a new form of window composition can be found in French stained glass of the 1260s and 1270s. The apse windows of the Cathedral of St Gatien of Tours depicting the bishops of Tours and the canons of Loches date from c.1260 and are the earliest surviving examples of the so-called 'band window' formula. Tall figures, singly or in pairs, stand in narrow compartments beneath simple canopies. The horizontal bands of coloured glass alternate with layers of foliage grisaille in which colour is used only very sparingly. A harmonious balance of colour and light is achieved. Although the Tours windows are the earliest 'band windows' to be preserved, it is clear that the formula was actually evolved in the Paris region; it was used in the earlier Lady Chapel windows of St

Germain-des-Prés in Paris, demolished between 1802 and 1805, and in the nave clerestory of St Denis in 1240–5.

The 'band window' did not immediately displace the earlier 'full colour' window typified by the legendary windows of Chartres or the Sainte Chapelle. At St Denis the band windows in the clerestory of the nave co-existed with the 'full colour' windows in the aisles; and in the glazing of Clermont Ferrand Cathedral, executed at much the same time as the bishops and canons windows at Tours, the older traditions of superimposed figurative compartments set within wide borders of saturated colour continued to be used.

Nor did the Tours formula represent the only approach to the problem of balancing colour and light in multi-light windows. In the church of St Pierre in Chartres, the tall lights of the choir clerestory contain alternating superimposed figures and foliage grisaille, while the nave windows contain-

**Above** The windows depicting the Canons of Loches and Bishops of Tours seen here in the choir clerestory of Tours Cathedral (c.1260) are the earliest examples of the new 'band window' approach to design, in which tiers of full colour alternate with tiers of light grisaille.

**Left** The canopies of c.1340–9 in the Lady Chapel of Ely Cathedral are unusual in their inclusion of peasant figures in their architectural niches.

ing large figures arrange them vertically in the centre of each light, with flanking strips of grisaille on either side. A similar central disposition of the coloured zone is found in the window given by Azon le Tort, a citizen of Rouen whose will of 1266 founded a chantry in the chapel of St Jean-jouxte-les-fonts in Rouen Cathedral, although the grisaille is a modern recreation of the original. In the clerestory windows of Cologne Cathedral dating from the first quarter of the fourteenth century, the light zone of grisaille glass is confined to the upper levels of the windows, with the lower panels reserved for figures under canopies. This is a particularly appropriate combination for extremely tall windows. A window of c.1270 dedicated to the Life of St Radegonde in the church of St Radegonde in Poitiers offers yet

**Right** The *Tapetenfenster* (carpet windows) in the Augustinian church in Erfurt (c.1300) are particularly decorative. On the south side the motifs are floral, while on the north side, parakeets, lions, fleurs-de-lis and floral wreaths are combined.

another formula: the figures are placed directly against a background of grisaille, an arrangement quite commonly found in early fourteenth-century stained glass in England, although in the English examples, such as the early fourteenth-century donor figures at Waterperry in Oxfordshire, the arrangement often appears to have been chosen for reasons of economy.

In the countries of the Empire, the 'lightening' of windows perceptible in France and England is far less apparent; here the taste for a richly coloured 'carpet-like' effect persisted throughout most of the fourteenth century, giving German windows a distinctive richness, which owed a great deal to the taste for tile-like background motifs in contrasting colours. This is true of the Blacksmith's window in the Cathedral of Freiburg im Breisgau, for example, where the figure and canopy formula is displayed against a dense trellis of colour.

This taste for a richly decorative effect is also manifest in windows of a non-figurative nature. *Tapetenfenster*, or carpet windows, are found in a number of German churches and cathedrals, such as Sankt Dionysius in Esslingen, and in those areas further east culturally indebted to Germany, in the castle chapel at Orlik in what is now Czechoslovakia, for example. It is thought that despite the importance of colour in these windows, they evolved from Cistercian grisaille designs of the thirteenth century, although the great height and narrow width of so many German windows, difficult to fill with figurative scenes, no doubt accounted for much of their popularity.

**Right** Henry de Mamesfeld displays remarkable self-importance in his glazing scheme for the chapel of Merton College. Although his 'portrait' figure is shown kneeling before images of the Apostles, his figure appears far more often than the saints he reveres (**opposite below**).

**Above** Queen Kunigunda, the patron saint of the donor Kunigunda Kropf, from the church of St Leonhard in Laventhal in Austria. The panel continues to use the decorative medallion to frame the figure, at a date (c.1340) when its use had ceased in France and England.

**Far right** In the chapel of St Catherine in Strasbourg Cathedral, constructed c.1340–5, the canopies dwarf the figures of the Apostles beneath.

One of the most imaginative of these carpet windows is to be found in the choir of the Augustinerkirche in Erfurt, where naturalistic foliage is combined with lions, garlands, fleurs-de-lis and parakeets. León Cathedral in Spain preserves a richly coloured vine window, conveying a similar effect, although this is a rather isolated example, making comparison difficult.

The figure and canopy formula which came to dominate fourteenth-century window design in England and France was less eagerly embraced by German glass-painters. Medallion frames persisted well into the fourteenth century, as in the Infancy cycle in the Barfüsserkirche and the St Augustine scenes in the Augustinerkirche in Erfurt, both dating from the first quarter of the century, where the scenes are framed by cusped quatrefoils, a device also favoured in the St Christina window of c.1330 in Regensburg Cathedral. The frames themselves evolved a range of elegant, sinuous forms, as in the Infancy window of c.1320 in the Frauenkirche in Esslingen. The elaborate 'keyhole' variety can be seen in the later glass depicting saints and donors from St Leonhard in Lavanthal in Austria (some of the panels of which are now in the Cloisters Museum in New York) and in panels of c.1350 depicting the story of Joachim and Anna at Regensburg.

The German city most receptive to French influence, and an important conduit for French influence in the Rhineland, was Strasbourg. The fourteenth-century windows in the cathedral use the figure and canopy formula to great effect, although the backgrounds employed are predominatly of richly coloured glass instead of the zones of grisaille favoured in England and France. Indeed, some of the Strasbourg canopies are of extraordinary delicacy and verticality, those in the St Catherine Chapel, for example, filling two-thirds of the tall narrow lights. Together with Cologne, the other German monument receptive to French ideas of Gothic, Strasbourg remained an enormously influential stylistic melting pot.

The donor achieves a new prominence in the stained glass of the fourteenth century. The role of the patron can never be underestimated, but from the closing years of the thirteenth century, the donor becomes a conspicuous physical presence in the window he or she had given. In the extraordinary choir windows of the chapel of Merton College in Oxford of c.1294, the donor, Henry de Mamesfeld, Fellow of the College, Chancellor of the University and subsequently Dean of Lincoln, appears twice in twelve out of the fourteen windows he donated, considerably outnumbering the Apostles he accompanies. Henry's figure is depicted on the same scale as the Apostles and he is identified by scrolls bearing the words '*Henricus de Mamesfeld Me Fecit*' (Henry de Mamesfeld had me made). Similar prominence is given to the figure of Raoul de Ferrières in his window of c.1325 in

the choir clerestory of Évreux Cathedral in Normandy. The life-size figure of the canon, finely dressed in a fur cape, kneels before the Virgin who suckles the Christ Child. The donor no longer looks like a dwarf at the feet of a giant, but convincingly like a person adoring the saintly personages in a real-life encounter.

This sense of communication between the mortal and the immortal, the worldly and the divine, is a subtle but essential hallmark of fourteenth-century art. The onlooker is invited to identify with the sacred drama. The humanity of Christ and his mother is emphasized, as is Christ's capacity for suffering on behalf of mankind. The Christ of the Crucifixion is the buffeted, broken corpse, the Virgin and St John at the foot of the Cross express human sorrow, a grief which is given heightened effect by the addition of the distraught Mary Magdalene, who clasps the foot of the Cross in abandoned grief, a motif derived from Italian exemplars. The single saint holding an emblem or attribute displaces in popularity the typological narrative, offering the worshipper an enormous number of devotional images to be turned to in times of distress and misfortune – St Margaret in childbirth, St Apollonia for toothache, St Christopher when travelling. Name saints were commonly chosen for inclusion in a donor's stained-glass window. It was above all the Virgin Mary whose intercession and protection was sought. The Virgin and Child group becomes an image of tenderness, as at Eaton Bishop in Herefordshire, and from the second quarter of the fourteenth century the Virgin Intercessor in scenes of the Last Judgment bares her breast to remind her son of her motherly love.

Evidence of patronage, particularly secular patronage of stained glass, is also frequently made manifest in the increasing prominence given to heraldic display. Heraldic devices figure in the repertoire of decorative motifs used to fill borders and tracery lights, although in this context they often have no precise heraldic significance. Many donor figures are dressed in heraldic surcoats or mantles, or support shields of arms decorated with identifying heraldic charges; in the choir of St Katherinerkirche in Oppenheim (Germany), twenty-two panels of c.1280 in the north-east choir window contain donor figures supporting shields. In many cases, however, heraldic display is substituted for the donor figure. This could be particularly useful in the case of an institutional donor – the patronage of the Freiburg blacksmiths, for example, is indicated by shields at the base of the window. A multiplicity of contributors to a single large commission could also be accommodated in a heraldic display, as in the east window of the Lady Chapel of Bristol Cathedral. Heraldry has the virtue of being extremely legible from a distance and could also be understood even by those unable to read labels and inscriptions.

The combination of refined elegance with a high degree of naturalism noted in the Raoul de Ferrières window is a characteristic of a group of works in stained glass belonging to what has been termed the 'Channel School', a loose description for a number of works sharing broad stylistic affinities found on both sides of the English Channel. In France this elegant work is found most plentifully in Normandy, particularly in Rouen and Évreux, and in England in the city of York, notably in the Minster, where it

**Opposite** In his window of c.1325 Canon Raoul de Ferrières in Évreux Cathedral offers the Virgin and Christ Child a model of his window, a device increasingly common in the fourteenth century. The Virgin is here represented as the earthly mother rather than the celestial queen.

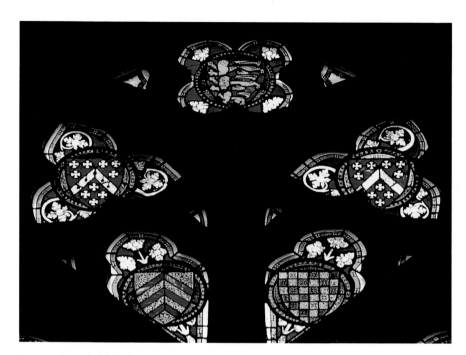

**Right** The upper tracery of the east window of the Lady Chapel at Bristol Cathedral (second quarter of the fourteenth century) demonstrates the legibility of medieval heraldry, even when viewed from a considerable distance.

is associated with the workshop of Master Robert, known to have been responsible for the west window of the nave.

An elegant refinement is not the only characteristic of this so-called 'Channel School'. There is also evidence of a nascent interest in the treatment of pictorial space, expressed as an imperfectly understood depiction of perspective. Although glass in this style does not survive in Paris, it is now recognized that its stylistic origins lie in the French capital and in the circle of the court. It is related to the style of the influential Parisian atelier of the illuminator Jean Pucelle, whose masterpiece, the 'Hours of Jeanne d'Évreux', was made c.1325–8 for the queen of Phillipe V. Pucelle's miniatures are filled with precocious 'doll's-house' structures. The source of this exciting new feature is to be found south of the Alps, exemplified by the enormous *Maesta* altarpiece by Duccio di Buoninsegna, made for Siena Cathedral and completed in 1311. Although it is thought that Pucelle may have designed small-scale architectural structures like shrines and so was familiar with work in the round, it is believed that he may actually have seen the *Maesta*. Italian panel paintings were also exported to northern Europe, providing northern artists with a new source of inspiration. A small number of East Anglian manuscripts dating from the 1330s and displaying Italianate features are evidence of the English response to the encounter with Italian art, and a panel of glass depicting the Annunciation in the nave of York Minster, probably by the workshop of Master Robert, reveals that this interest was not confined to the art of the book.

An interest in perspectival effect can be seen in stained glass other than that of England and France. In those countries sharing borders with Italy, experimentation with spatial effects was early and sophisticated. One of the most remarkable sets of windows displaying these features in a well-developed form is found in the church at Koenigsfelden, in the canton of Aargau in Switzerland. On 1 May 1308, the Hapsburg King Albrecht I was murdered in a family feud by his nephew John of Swabia. The dowager

**Above**  The Hours of Jeanne d'Évreux, made for the Queen of France c.1325, is the work of the illuminator Jean Pucelle. Its miniatures combine extreme delicacy and refinement with a precocious interest in spatial perspective and a taste for marginal 'drolleries'.

**Above left**  In this annunciation in York Minster (c.1340) the workshop of Master Robert has attempted to place the scene within a convincing architectural space, an idea absorbed from Sienese art.

Queen Elizabeth founded Koenigsfelden for the spiritual well-being of her murdered husband and for the Hapsburg family. After 1311 it was occupied by six Franciscans, who were soon joined by a community of Poor Clares. The nunnery expanded enormously and from 1317 was protected and guided by Queen Elizabeth's widowed daughter Agnes. Agnes did not take the veil but was revered as a 'wonderfully shrewd, quick-witted woman, with the courage of a man', and under her rule the community flourished. The church was built between 1310 and 1330 and is typical of the barn-like constructions favoured by the Grey Friars, being ideal for preaching to large congregations.

The glory of the Koenigsfelden choir is undoubtedly its stained glass, depicting the Incarnation and Passion of Christ, and the Lives of Saints John the Baptist, Elizabeth of Thuringia, Catherine, Anne, Paul and Nicholas. Windows were also devoted to the Lives of St Francis and St Clare. The windows were given by members of King Albrecht's family, who appear in them as donor figures. On the basis of the patronal evidence, the windows can be dated to a single glazing programme of c.1325–30 and were the

**Right** The Beheading of St John the Baptist at Koenigsfelden in Switzerland (*c*.1325) unfolds on a projecting platform. The prison from which St John's figure emerges has believable substance, although the perspective of its upper storeys is not entirely successful.

work of a single workshop.

The narrative unfolds on projecting platforms that appear to hover against deeply coloured decorative backgrounds. Several incidents take place within or in front of elaborate architectural structures: the beheading of St John the Baptist, for example, is set outside a multi-storeyed prison, while in the scene of the stigmatization of St Francis, a fine three-dimensional church stands to the right. Interior spaces are articulated in contrasting colours and white glass is used in thin strips, borders and fillets to provide a sparkling counterpoint to the richness of the colour.

An even more highly developed version of 'doll's-house' architecture is found in panels of slightly later date from the pilgrimage church of Strassengel near Graz in Styria (Austria), now in the Victoria and Albert Museum. The church was consecrated in 1353 and the glass, of roughly this date, is stylistically related to glass in the choir of St Stephen's Cathedral in

Vienna. The scenes of the Life of the Virgin are perched on platforms that support towering multi-tiered canopies. As in the Koenigsfelden windows, contrasting colour is used to enhance the sense of spatial complexity. The Koenigsfelden and Strassengel windows show that glass-painters of the Hapsburg territories were familiar with the fresco cycles of northern Italy and particularly the achievements of Giotto and his circle. In both instances the sense of spatial recession is limited, however, by the continued use of flat backgrounds of deep colour in repetitive tile patterns, which prevent the eye from straying beyond the two-dimensional picture plane. This apparent contradiction between the three-dimensional foreground and the flat backround remained unresolved until the late fourteenth-century introduction of landscape.

In Italy the fresco and the painted altarpiece continued to be the premier form of monumental painting, although material for a history of glass-

**Above**   The mid fourteenth-century Presentation of the Virgin Mary, from Strassengel in Austria, depicted beneath artificially complex canopies, is now in the Victoria and Albert Museum in London.

**Left**   In this scene, in which St Francis is miraculously transported to hear the eloquence of St Anthony of Padua, a Sienese glass-painter reveals his familiarity with the style of the famous Giotto.

**Above** The early fourteenth-century tracery lights of the Lucy Chapel of Christ Church Cathedral, Oxford, contain a number of amusing and irreverent hybrid creatures, which appear alongside conventional religious subjects.

painting becomes more plentiful. In the thirteenth century the church at Assisi had attracted German glaziers to work in the upper basilica – the Franciscan church in Erfurt had been one of the first to depict the Life of St Francis in stained glass. In the lower basilica, the artist reponsible for the window recounting the Life of St Anthony of Padua reveals his familiarity with the work of Giotto, not only in the articulation of convincing architectural structures, but also in the plasticity and solidity of his forms and his talent as a story-teller. The glass-painters worked closely with fresco-painters, and the schemes for windows and walls were closely integrated, sometimes being designed by a single artist, as in the chapel of St Martin in the lower basilica where Simone Martini was probably personally responsible for the glass and the mural decoration. In the Baroncelli Chapel in Santa Croce in Florence, the author of the stained glass was Taddeo Gaddi, the artist responsible for the frescoes of c.1340. At both Assisi and at Santa Croce it is unlikely that the fresco-painters also painted the glass. In Italy it was far commoner for glass-painters to be supplied with cartoons to work from than it was north of the Alps. As a result, the trecento achievements in the depiction of a naturalistically conceived pictorial space were quickly translated into stained glass, giving Italian windows a solemn monumentalism and a spatial sophistication rarely matched north of the Alps.

Against this backdrop of greater naturalism in stained glass, the glass-painter's delight in the depiction of the grotesque 'drolleries' and 'babewyns' of fable and imagination seems perverse and contradictory. Even in the elegant 'Hours of Jeanne d'Évreux' and the equally courtly 'Queen Mary Psalter', the margins and *bas de page* are filled with light-hearted embellishments drawn from a variety of secular literature, bestiaries and the imagination of the artist. While the more structured format of a window opening offered fewer outlets for this kind of artistic exuberance, creatures of a grotesque and fantastic nature can still be found in stained glass. The windows in St Ouen in Rouen, which, as we have seen, were strongly influenced by the art of Jean Pucelle, contain medallions with amusing 'babewyns'. Satirical and irreverent hybrids fill the tracery lights of the Lucy Chapel and contorted beasts fill the borders of the Latin Chapel in Oxford Cathedral, while the bottom border of the Pilgrimage window of York Minster recounts the fable of Reynard the Fox.

Of almost equal importance to the design changes evolving in the early fourteenth century are the technological developments that contributed to the transformation. Improvements in glass manufacture made available larger, thinner sheets of glass of a brighter, clearer quality. Contact with the Islamic east was responsible for the most important technical innovation in stained glass of the Middle Ages. By the mid thirteenth century a recipe for yellow stain, a technique known to the Egyptians, had been translated from Arabic into Castilian and was included in *El Lapidario*, a work compiled by the humanist king of Castile, Alfonso X. A copy of this influential text had reached the court of France by the end of the thirteenth century, and by the first decade of the fourteenth century this revolutionary colouring technique was being employed in France and England, although it appeared in Castile at a later date.

Yellow stain, a colour which could be applied with the brush (see p. 26), was to have far-reaching effects on the history of glass-painting. It has proved impossible to date its earliest use with great precision. In 1943 the French glass historian Jean Lafond suggested that the glass at Le Mesnil-Villeman (Manche) was the earliest firmly datable example (1313) of its use, based on an inscription in the glass. It is inconceivable, however, that this technique was unknown to Parisian glass-painters, particularly those working close to the court. The loss of so much glass in Paris leaves a gap in our unravelling of the history of its glass-painters. The 'Heraldic Window' in York Minster, datable to c.1307–10, is almost certainly the earliest surviving English example, although the loss of so much in London has no doubt distorted the picture in much the same way as it has for Parisian glass-painting history. Peter de Dene, the donor of the window was a cosmopolitan figure, and York itself was at the heart of English cultural and political life in the early fourteenth century, when the king and his court spent protracted periods there during the prosecution of the Scottish wars.

A combination of warfare, iconoclasm, pestilence and political unrest means that relatively little stained glass survives from the period 1350–1400. A detailed history of this phase of European glass-painting remains to be written, although it is clear that it was a period of a rapidly evolving naturalism in both painting and sculpture. A more consistent and perceptive use of three-dimensional architectural forms was accompanied by a more credible modelling of the human form and the beginnings of genuine characterization in the depiction of faces. Courtly elegance gives way to the vigour of a somewhat coarsened 'transitional style', which was quickly evolved into a softer, more painterly style. This is nowhere better displayed than in the glass commissioned by William of Wykeham (Bishop of Winchester and Chancellor of England) for New College in Oxford, glazed

**Above** The so-called 'Heraldic Window' in the nave aisle of York Minster was given c.1307–10 by Canon Peter de Dene. The sophisticated glass-painting workshop responsible has used the new technique of yellow stain to decorate the heraldic surcoat, the sword-buckler and spurs. Small splashes have also dropped onto the king's chain-mail sleeves.

c.1380–6 by the workshop of Thomas Glazier. The windows of the antechapel combine great delicacy of decorative detail with a vigorous figure style and an element of strong characterization. Robust figures with prominent features stand beneath tangibly solid canopies surmounted by 'pepper-pot' turrets and finials. In the later work by this same workshop, for Wykeham's Winchester College, the harsher, harder aspects of this style have been softened and the painterly qualities enhanced. In the fragments of the Jesse Tree from the east window the figures are positioned in the foliage of a fleshy vine, and twist, turn and gesture in a variety of poses.

This 'soft' style is the hallmark of 'International Gothic' painting, which as its name suggests, can be found throughout late fourteenth-century Europe. In England it has now been recognized at Exeter (the east window of the Cathedral), at Canterbury (the west window of the Cathedral) and at York (the western choir clerestory of the Minster), all dating from the last quarter of the century. The famous Duc Jean de Berry, best known for his sumptuous *Trés Riches Heures*, also commissioned stained glass for the

**Above** In the much restored glass in Winchester College Chapel, executed in a softer style, William of Wykeham, donor of the glass at both Winchester and New College, kneels before the Virgin Mary, to whom both his colleges were dedicated. His head is a modern copy of a medieval 'portrait' head elsewhere in the window.

**Right** The facial characterization of this saint in the antechapel of New College, Oxford, is typical of the hard, transitional style of the late fourteenth century. The almost sculptural treatment of the nose, mouth and eyes creates a startlingly realistic image.

**Left** The distinctive canopies of the New College windows are filled with tiny traceried windows, delicately enlivened with yellow stain.

**Below** The sumptuous glazing commissioned by Jean, Duc de Berry for his Sainte-Chapelle in Bourges (now in the crypt of Bourges Cathedral) illustrates many of the stylistic trends found in Wykeham's glass. Although the master glass-painter's name is unknown, the strong influence of the court painter André Beauneveu can be detected in many of the figures.

Sainte-Chapelle attached to his palace at Bourges. This chapel was destroyed in 1757, but some of its glass survives in the crypt of Bourges Cathedral. The glass was executed between c.1395 and 1405, when the chapel was consecrated. The identity of the glass-painters responsible is unknown, although it has been suggested that the atelier worked under the direction of André Beauneveu, the painter in the duke's service from c.1385 responsible for the volumetric and softly draped figures in the 'Psalter of Jean de Berry' in the Bibliothèque National. Some of the Bourges figures, part of a Creed series, are remarkably close to Beauneveu's work, while others represent a harder style. Startling comparisons can be made between the New College and Bourges figures, highlighting the truly international flavour of late fourteenth-century painting.

# FROM LATE GOTHIC TO RENAISSANCE AND REFORMATION

By the end of the fourteenth century, the glass-painter, for so long a largely anonymous figure, begins to emerge from obscurity, and the surviving work of identifiable glass-painters can at last be studied. At Winchester College, the glass-painter Master Thomas Glazier is included among 'portrait' figures of the early 1390s in the east window of the chapel. This evidence becomes even more plentiful in the course of the fifteenth and early sixteenth centuries. In early fifteenth-century York the work of John Thornton can be identified in the Minster and by stylistic comparison in the city's parish churches; in sixteenth-century Metz Valentin Busch emerges as the leading glass-painter, initialling many of his windows, while in Beauvais the work of Engrand Le Prince can be identified by the appearance of a signature in his remarkable Jesse window of c.1525 for the church of Saint-Etienne. The bearded young king on whose sleeve the initials 'ENGR' are painted is probably a realistic image of the artist himself.

It is even possible to begin to piece together the careers of some of these artists. Peter Hemmel von Andlau, for example, born c.1420, founded his fortune on an advantageous marriage to the widow of a master glass-painter in Strasbourg. His business prospered and from 1475 to 1476 he served as a magistrate. The Flemish glass-painter Arnoult of Nijmegen was a native of Tournai, where he was responsible for a series of windows in the Cathedral on the histories of Kings Chilperic and Sigebert. In 1502 he moved to Rouen where he worked until 1513, signing a number of windows and revitalizing glass-painting in the city.

The same period also witnessed the increasing formalization of craft

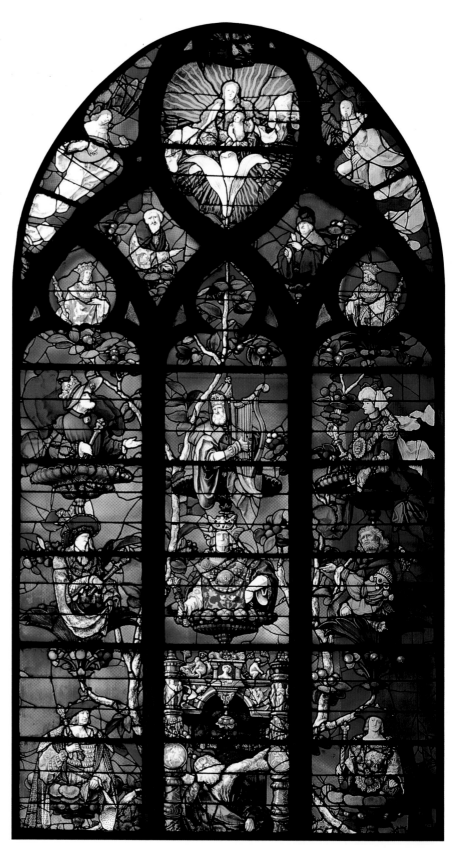

**Right** The church of St Etienne in Beauvais contains this sumptuous Jesse Tree by Engrand Le Prince, whose initials appear on the sleeve of the bearded young king in the right-hand light.

organization throughout Europe. The medieval guilds were the bodies responsible for the regulation of the crafts, and guild ordinances were formulated in London (1364–5), York (1463–4), Paris (1467), Lyon (1496) and Vienna. A study of the surviving texts reveals that serious attempts were made to preserve standards, regulate admission to the craft by limiting apprentice numbers and charging fees to those setting up new businesses, and to establish training procedures. In some cities – Prague, Antwerp and Tournai, for example – the glass-painters joined the Guild of St Luke which represented painters in a variety of media. In both England and France the post of glazier to the Crown emerged as the most important and lucrative appointment. Although such a post had probably existed in an informal and temporary sense since the thirteenth century, under Richard II of England and Charles VI of France it became a position of greater permanence and status. From 1390 the personnel of the French court included a 'peintre du Roi' and in 1378 the former master of the London Glaziers Company, John de Brampton, became 'King's Glazier within the Tower of London, the Palace of Westminster and all his other castles and manors'. By 1440, John Prudde was not only receiving a salary and a gown of the king's livery, but also enjoying the use of a sizeable workshop within the Westminster Palace complex, identified as 'a shedde called the glasyer logge'. The most valuable English glazing commission on record was for the king; in 1402 William Burgh was paid 3s 4d per foot for decorative glazing with emblems and mottoes for King Henry IV's private apartments at Eltham Palace. Almost half a century later John Prudde

**Above** The east window of the Beauchamp chapel in St Mary's church in Warwick is the only documented work by the King's Glazier, John Prudde, to have survived. Using only the finest imported glass, and filled with 'jewels', this window, commissioned in 1447, expresses the rich tastes of the English court.

**Left** The Annunciation window in Bourges Cathedral, commissioned c.1448 by the silversmith Jacques Coeur, illustrates a similar taste for rich colour and jewelled decoration. Coeur's enormous wealth gave him access to the leading glass-painters of the day, employed elsewhere by royal patrons.

received only 2s per foot for the sumptuous glazing of the Beauchamp Chapel in Warwick. This is all that survives of Prudde's large body of work documented in royal records; his glazing for Henry VI has disappeared. King René of Anjou employed André Robin as his court painter, and stained glass by him has survived in the two rose windows of Angers Cathedral and in an Apostles Creed series in Quimper Cathedral.

The newly rich mercantile classes emerged as important patrons of glaziers. Numerous windows in the parish churches of cities like York, Norwich, Bourges, Rouen, Nuremburg and Cologne were glazed at the behest of a class of men and women who owed wealth and social prominence not to aristocratic birth but to business acumen and commer-

**Right** Browne's Hospital in Stamford (Lincolnshire) was founded by a wealthy wool-merchant, William Browne, whose personal badge and motto appear at the base of the left-hand light. This glazing programme of the 1470s is the principal surviving work by a workshop active in the Peterborough area.

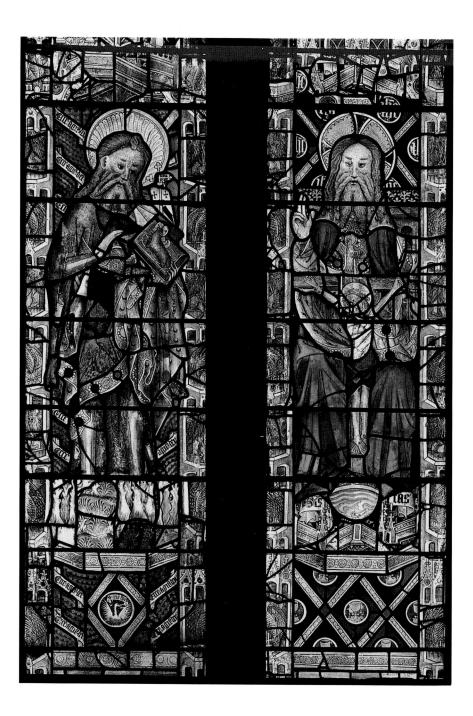

cial enterprise. In France the Bourges silversmith Jacques Coeur donated the exquisite Annunciation window in the Cathedral (c.1448), which was executed by the leading Bourges workshop of the day also employed by the Duc de Berry in both his capital and at the Sainte-Chapelle at Riom in the Auvergne. In Stamford in Lincolnshire a charitable hospital was founded and richly glazed out of the bequests of William Browne, a merchant of the Staple (wool), who died in 1489. Preserved in the Musées Royaux d'Art et d'Histoire in Brussels is a series of five fine early sixteenth-century heraldic panels, originating in the Hospital of Saint Elizabeth in Lierre, probably commemorating the wealthy benefactors of the hospital.

Private chapels in the homes of the wealthy were often glazed, but in the fifteenth century stained glass was increasingly widely used in secular and domestic settings, although relatively little has survived. The domestic ranges of monastic foundations were glazed or partially glazed from an early date, but the homes of lay people also provided the glazier with work. Heraldic display against a background of quarry glazing was a popular and practical formula for a great hall or solar. Ockwells Manor House in Berkshire, built between 1446 and 1466 by Sir John Norreys, preserves *in situ* eighteen shields of arms in the narrow-mullioned windows of its hall. In 1505 Lady Margaret Beaufort had problems with her glazier, who was working on heraldic glazing for her hall at Collyweston Manor; John Delyon had depicted the heraldic yale as a common antelope and the mistake had to be remedied at the cost of 7s. Small figurative roundels were also popular in domestic contexts; Roger Wyggeston's house in Leicester preserved a number of them in its narrow timber-framed windows (now in Leicester Museum). The roundel was ideal in the intimate setting of the private chamber where its delicate detail could be appreciated with ease. Those stories that could be told in a series of related incidents were well suited for display in the multiple, generally narrow openings of late fifteenth-

**Right** The Mérode Altarpiece of *c.*1425 by the Master of Flemalle depicts a religious subject, the Annunciation to the Virgin Mary, within a domestic interior that would have been familiar to the bourgeois donors kneeling in the left-hand wing.

and early sixteenth-century windows. Religious subjects were common, even for the domestic interior, although the Labours of the Months depicting a series of rural occupations, and Biblical stories with plenty of lively, if not racy detail – Susanna and the Elders and the Prodigal Son, for example – were also popular. The distinctive late fifteenth-century quatre-foil leaded roundels produced by German glass-painters belonging to the circle of the so-called Master of the Housebook included scenes of hunting, jousting and feasting. Some impression of the way in which roundels were used can be gleaned from contemporary panel paintings depicting domestic interiors. These show that window openings were generally divided into two by transoms. The lower two-thirds of the window, often containing an unglazed lattice, were shuttered, while the upper third might contain a roundel within a border set into plain quarries. An actual glazing programme can be reconstructed from a nineteenth-century drawing for the house at 9 Pieterskerkgracht, in Leiden, the home of the bailiff of Rijnland, Adriaen Dircxz. van Crimpen. Three double-light, oak window frames were installed in an upstairs hall. The window mullions, two of which survive, were themselves elaborately carved, and the glass, executed by Dirck Crabeth and his workshop in 1543, combined roundels of Samuel and the Life of St Paul with architectural ornament.

There is some evidence that civic and public buildings were occasionally furnished with stained glass. About 1420 the town hall of Luneburg in Germany was glazed with depictions of the Nine Heroes taken from pagan, Jewish and Christian history. The Merchant's Guildhall at Coventry (Warwickshire), St Mary's Hall, was provided in about 1500 with a splendid window depicting a series of kings of England, although as the headquarters of the influential Trinity Guild, the hall also fulfilled a quasi-religious function. On a less grandiose scale, market halls and judicial chambers might be glazed with heraldry and simple painted quarries, of the type surviving in the mayor's parlour in Leicester. Merchant's marks, monograms, flowers, birds, grotesques and drolleries would all have provided suitable motifs.

The personal reputations of individual glass-painters could be considerable. Throughout the Middle Ages, the easiest way for any patron to express his personal preferences was to request that his commission should resemble another specified work of art. In the fifteenth century this could also mean seeking out the services of specific renowned artists. The glass-painter John Thornton of Coventry was invited to York in 1405 to work on the east window of the Minster; he had probably been brought to the attention of the dean and chapter by Archbishop Scrope, who had no doubt become familiar with Thornton's Coventry achievements while he was Bishop of nearby Lichfield. A more impressive example of reputation preceding the man is furnished by the career of the Frenchman Guillaume de Marcillat. Born in 1467, he entered the Dominican house in Nevers, but in 1506 was invited to Rome by Pope Julius II, where he worked at the Vatican alongside Bramante and Michelangelo. He continued his Italian career in Arezzo, where he became acquainted with the biographer Vasari, who praised the work of 'il Marcilla' very highly. One of the most renowned fifteenth-century glass-painters was Peter Hemmel. His Strasbourg work-shop provided glass for a number of the city's churches, of which only one remains *in situ*, but his fame was such that his workshop supplied glass for Freiburg im Breisgau Cathedral, Munich, Nuremburg, Ulm and Salzburg.

**Left**  The Nine Heroes depicted in stained glass of *c*.1420 in the town hall at Luneburg in Germany are derived from the courtly poem *The Vows of the Peacock*, in which they represent the epitome of courage and perseverance.

Links between the courts of Europe facilitated mobility among artists; the most important glazier in Toledo from 1485 to 1492 was Enrique Aleman, while the Fleming Barnard Flower became king's glazier to Henry VII and Henry VIII. Flower, who had formerly been in the service of the Duke of Burgundy, probably first came to England in the duke's entourage during a diplomatic embassy in 1496.

Some small evidence emerges for a devolution of functions within the glazing workshop during the fifteenth century. This affected in particular the respective roles of the 'glass-painter' and the glass 'craftsman', which became more distinct. In late fifteenth-century Norwich, for example, the workshop of Thomas Goldbeater contained two apprentice glaziers and one apprentice painter, William Heyward, who by 1505 had become an independent master. The enormous increase in demand for simple domestic glazing no doubt helped to foster the distinction between the artistic medium and its more prosaic counterpart. The use of paper was to revolutionize the working methods of the medieval glazing workshop and facilitated the exchange of ideas and motifs between artists working in different media. In 1447 John Prudde received from the executors of the will of Richard Beauchamp 'patterns of paper' to serve as the basis for the windows in the Beauchamp Chapel. A series of twenty-four early sixteenth-century preparatory drawings for stained glass in Brussels has recently been attributed to the patronage of Cardinal Wolsey and identified as the work of the Nuremburg artist Erhard Schön, which was to be translated into glass in England. The changing relationship between designers and craftsmen in

**Right** The Annunciation and the Nativity in one of twenty-four *vidimuses* prepared by the studio of Erhard Schön, probably designed for Cardinal Wolsey's new chapel at Hampton Court.

the later Middle Ages is revealed by a comparison of the working practices in the Nuremburg workshops of Michael Wolgemut and Veit Hirschvogel the Elder. In the studio of Wolgemut, where Dürer trained as a young man, members of the atelier were involved in every stage of the execution of the workshop's stained-glass commissions. Dürer and his pupils, on the other hand, produced numerous designs for stained glass, but were not involved in their technical execution. A number of designs on paper for stained glass by Hans Suess von Kulmbach and Hans Baldung Grien have survived, most of which were executed by the workshop of Veit Hirsvogel the Elder and his sons, Veit the Younger and Hans. Their most important collaboration was in the glazing of the cloister of the Nuremburg Carmelite monastery between 1504 and 1510. The delicate hatched modelling of the figures recalls the style of the graphic source. While this sort of artistic exchange could be extremely beneficial, it also tended, in the long run, to lead to the diminution of the status of the glass-painter and an emphasis on his craft skills above his original creative talents. In Italy this was certainly to be the case; by the late fourteenth century, Cennino Cennini, in his *Craftsman's Handbook*, had already accepted that design and execution are separate functions and he advises the master glass-painter to seek the assistance of a draughtsman in the preparation of his designs, describing how sheets of paper might be joined to make the cartoon. In Europe north of the Alps the prestige of the medium was such that it continued to attract artists who were not glass specialists. It has been argued, with some conviction, that glass of the 1470s in the church of Notre-Dame-La-Riche in Tours is the work of Jean Fouquet, a native of Tours and the most renowned French painter of his day, who was commissioned by kings and princes and has hitherto been known primarily as a painter of miniatures and panels.

The soft, painterly conventions of International Gothic were long-lived in

**Above left** Death on horseback, a design for stained glass produced c.1502 by the so-called Benedict Master, an artist in the circle of Albrecht Dürer. Plague was raging in Europe at the time, and the grisly image of death is a warning to the living.

**Above** The design as executed in glass by the workshop of Veit Hirsvogel the Elder. Death aims at a companion panel (not illustrated) depicting Dr Sixtus Tucher, and warns him 'Beware, unfortunate one, that I do not lay you, pierced by my arrow, on this hard bed of the funeral bier'.

**Right**   The Virgin Mary weaves the curtain of the Temple in this panel by the workshop of Veit Hirsvogel, made between 1504 and 1510 for the Carmelite cloister in Nuremburg. The panel was probably designed by Hans Baldung Grien.

fifteenth-century Europe north of the Alps, lasting until the mid century in some areas. The work by John Glazier of the 1440s at All Souls College, Oxford, for example, differs relatively little from the 'soft' style work by Thomas Glazier of the 1390s at New College and Winchester College. In the fifteenth century naturalism was to give way to an increased realism; painters now held up a mirror to the real world, and stained glass thus becomes an increasingly valuable document of social history, offering numerous glimpses of the world in which its creators lived and worked. The sacred narrative was conceived more often in terms of a contemporary medieval setting, encouraging the observer to identify and empathize with the devotional image. This tendency is highly developed in the work of the Netherlandish painter of the Mérode altarpiece (c.1427), the so-called Master of Flemalle, sometimes identified as the Tournai artist Robert Campin. The Annunciation to the Virgin Mary (see p. 94) takes place in the interior of a bourgeois town house filled with the implements of everyday life. The activity of the town goes on beyond the open window and the kneeling donor figures peer in on the sacred scene through a partially open door that creates a physical link between the main panel and its flanking wing. The depiction of the real world in most stained glass of the first half of the fifteenth century is more superficial, although characters are frequently dressed in contemporary costume, and the all-purpose diaphanous robes are less universal. In John Thornton's east window of York Minster (1405–8), Noah's wife wears a fashionable beaded headdress, while the family dog perches excitedly on the stern of the ark, which is depicted as a fifteenth-century merchant ship. John Glazier's female saints at All Souls are similarly fashionably clad. In the Adoration of the Magi (c.1420) in the east window of the Staufberg church in Switzerland, the three kings sport figure-hugging doublets with scalloped sleeves, while one wears particoloured hose. Donor figures offer the most fruitful evidence of contemporary fashion, particularly valuable as so many funeral effigies and brasses on which they also appear have lost all traces of polychromy.

The depiction of the human form also undergoes a change at this time. In both John Thornton's naked Adam in the east window of York Minster (1405–8) and in Peter Hemmel's Adam of c.1470 from the destroyed

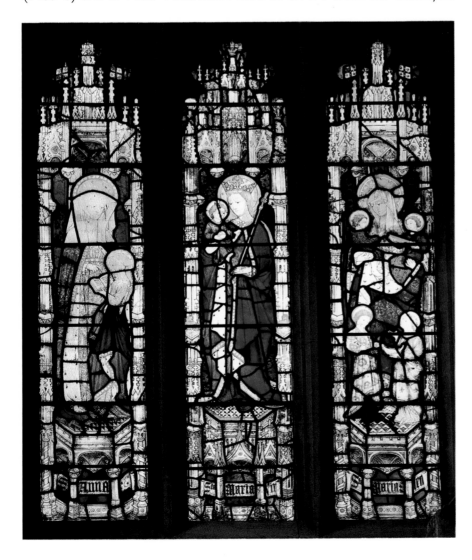

**Left** Fashionably-clad female saints, by the workshop of John Glazier in the antechapel at All Souls College, Oxford. Glazier was paid for the antechapel windows in 1447.

**Above** The realistic figure of the naked Adam, revelling in the lush foliage of the Garden of Eden, was made c.1470 by the workshop of Peter Hemmel for the destroyed church of St Pierre-le-Vieux in Strasbourg, and is now in the Musée de l'Oeuvre Notre Dame.

church of Saint-Pierre-le-Vieux in Strasbourg, there is evidence of a greater interest in and understanding of the human anatomy. Bland facial formulas are replaced by a sometimes startling degree of characterization, suggesting that the artist's observation of his surroundings is being translated directly into his work. This is manifest in the vigorous and even coarsened features of some of Thornton's characters, in which the psychology of the narrative is explored in the physiognomy of the individual. Thornton's ingenuity in depicting the more difficult aspects of the book of Revelation in stained glass reveals him to have been a designer and artist of exceptional talent. The donor portrait of Dr Lorenz Tucher from the Michaelskirche in Fürth, painted by the workshop of Michael Wolgemut in 1485, has the feeling of being an accurate depiction of Tucher's actual appearance. He is portrayed in the clerical dress of a rector. The fur almuce over his shoulders identifies him as Provost of the Lorenzkirche in Nuremburg. The conventional donor portrait has been transformed by a quality of realism.

Although fifteenth-century glass-painters employed perspectival devices in the depiction of the architectural components of their windows, they were relatively slow to dispense with the conventions of an earlier era, wisely recognizing that theirs was a two-dimensional medium. They continued to arrange their narrative against richly coloured, flat, diapered backgrounds. In the heavily restored glass of c.1408 in the church of St Martin at Hal (Belgium), the softly modelled, sculptural figures of Christ, the Virgin Mary and saints are positioned under complex, overhanging canopies filled with inhabited niches with projecting roofs and shuttered windows. Yet realism is curtailed by the use behind figures and architecture alike of flat, chequered backgrounds, which come down like a curtain, cutting off further spatial recession.

Only in the second half of the fifteenth century do glass-painters begin to abandon the rigid framing of scenes under Gothic architectural canopies, a standard feature of stained glass since the last decade of the thirteenth century, in favour of a freer treatment of the picture space. In Jacques Coeur's Bourges window, for example, it is apparent that the glass-painter no longer feels constrained by the rigid divisions of the architecture of the window opening. The Annunciation takes place under a spangled vault which spans two lights of the window, ignoring the intervening mullions. Over the top of a rich hanging draped behind the figures, the observer glimpses the windows of the chapels beyond. In the beautiful Coronation of the Virgin window in St Gommaire in Lierre, dating from the third quarter of the fifteenth century, the designer has exiled the architectural components to the very edges of his window. The Virgin is crowned within a splendid cloud-rimmed 'capsule' in the middle of the window, which cuts across the mullions. Christ and God the Father, who with the dove of the Holy Spirit are in the act of crowning the Virgin, stretch across the confines of the lights in order to place the crown on her head. The use of a large quantity of white glass gives the figures a sculptural look, enhanced by the soft stippled modelling. In the Rieter window in the church of St Lorenz in Nuremburg, the architectural canopies are pushed out to the outer extremities of the window and several of the scenes, the grapes of Eschol and the Plague of Flies, for example, unfold across two lights, ignoring the intervening mullions. In Peter Hemmel's panels the architecture takes on an organic, foliar quality and becomes more and more insubstantial, although it is not abandoned altogether. None of these late fifteenth-century northern Gothic glass-painters could quite bring themselves to set their figures in a fully conceived landscape or spacious interior, and the diapered background continued to be widely used until the end of the century, contradicting the

**Top**  John Thornton's imaginative depiction of the four winds in the east window of York Minster.

**Above**  The worried brow of Cain, who has just murdered his brother Abel in the east window of York Minster.

**Left**  Dr Lorenz Tucher, provost of the Lorenzkirche in Nuremburg. In 1485, he was 38 years old, and this panel has the quality of a genuine portrait.

**Right** The late fifteenth-century Coronation of the Virgin in the church of St Gommaire in Lierre (Belgium) reveals the pervasive influence of the painter Rogier van der Weyden.

apparent reality of the foreground.

In Italy stained glass followed rather different lines of development. As we have seen, glass-painters participated in the experimentation in the depiction of pictorial space at an early date, as exemplified by the St Francis windows at Padua. In Mariotto di Nardo's Life of St James window of c.1410 in San Domenico in Perugia, a number of the scenes take place in the open air. The landscape is formed out of rather artificial rocky 'layers', and figures and clusters of buildings are juxtaposed in an uneasy combination. The scenes are set not against decorative diaper, however, but against a blue sky. Leading painters and sculptors continued to supply the cartoons from which the glass-painters worked. In the glazing of Florence Cathedral,

**Left**   The Circumcision of Christ (c.1450) by Domenico Ghirlandaio, in the apse of Santa Maria Novella in Florence. The temple is depicted as a classical basilica with a coffered ceiling.

for example, the sculptor and goldsmith Lorenzo Ghiberti (c.1378–1455), famed for his bronze doors for the Florence Baptistery, provided cartoons for at least twenty windows, seventeen of which are documented. These include three of the occuli in the west front, starting with the Assumption of the Virgin, installed in 1405. Paolo Uccello, one of Ghiberti's pupils, supplied the cartoons for the Nativity occulus. In the 1440s both artists, together with Andrea del Castagno and Donatello, supplied cartoons for the eight occuli in the dome, one of which has since been lost. In Ghiberti's Garden of Gethsemane, Christ and the sleeping Apostles are positioned in a plausible landscape with the walls and rooftops of the city in the background. Although these Florentine windows have suffered disturbance, indifferent

**Above** Christ and the Woman Taken in Adultery in Arezzo Cathedral, by Guilluame de Marcillat. 'These are not windows', wrote the awed Vasari, 'but marvels fallen from heaven for the consolation of men'.

restoration and pigment loss, they have a monumental quality and an assurance in the manipulation of the human form in three-dimensional pictorial space which reflects the sculptural experience of their designers. Surrounded by tangible reminders of their great Roman past, Italian artists of the fifteenth century, like their architect colleagues, naturally employed classical architectural forms. In Domenico Ghirlandaio's apse windows for Santa Maria Novella in Florence (c.1450), Christ's Circumcision takes place in a temple with a classical coffered vault supported by classical columns. In Cristoforo de Mottis's Life of St John window in Milan Cathedral (1478), scenes take place in a fully fledged classical cityscape, while the fertile surrounding countryside is glimpsed beyond the city's edge. Despite this pictorial splendour, Italian stained-glass artists appear generally to have been held in rather lower esteem than their northern colleagues, and techniques of glass-painting and glazing were less advanced. Silver stain, extensively used in northern Europe since the beginning of the fourteenth century, makes its first appearance in Italy only in the first decade of the fifteenth; the earliest surviving example is in the work of Mariotto di Nardo at Perugia. The rise to prominence of the Frenchman Guillaume de Marcillat marked the end of the phase of native glass-painting in Italy. During the rest of the sixteenth century, the art was to be dominated by expatriate Germans and Flemings, notably Konrad Much (De Mochis) from Cologne and Valerius Diependale from Louvain, both of whom held the post of chief glazier at Milan Cathedral.

From the last quarter of the fifteenth century, stained glass moved into the full stream of the Renaissance; a continuing contact with Italy, in stained glass as in other media, was of great importance. In Germany in the middle years of the fifteenth century an important technical invention provided the means of spreading new pictorial models and stylistic trends throughout Europe. From the late fourteenth century, woodcuts had enabled simple pictures to be printed from relief-carved blocks. Woodcuts were used to decorate cheap consumer goods like playing cards and could also be combined with hand-written texts. From c.1450 blocks were cut with both illustration and text to create simple printed books, called block-books. The most popular and widely disseminated block-book was the *Biblia Pauperum* or *Poor Man's Bible*, first produced in the Netherlands in about 1464–5. The block-book offered forty pages of text and image arranged in a typological sequence and provided a direct model for the Bible scenes in the choir at Holy Trinity Tattershall (glazed 1466–80) and for the sixteenth-century glazing for the Cistercian Abbey of Mariawald near Cologne. The hard-edged, linear quality of this kind of illustration even began to influence the way in which glass-painters modelled their figures (see p. 105).

At about the same time as the block-book appeared, artists seeking a more subtle effect developed copper-plate engraving, the negative of the wood-block, which is a form of relief printing. Much finer lines could be achieved in the copper plate, which also had a far longer life. One of the greatest exponents of copper-plate engraving was Martin Schöngauer, but Dürer, the genius of the late fifteenth- and early sixteenth-century Nuremburg, worked extensively in both woodcuts and copper-plate

**Left** Goliath slain by David, from Holy Trinity, Tattershall (Lincolnshire), glazed 1466–80.

**Top** The same scene in the block-book *Biblia Pauperum*, designed in the Netherlands *c.*1465. In the block-book it appears, together with Samson and the Lion, as a type of Christ liberating the righteous from Limbo.

**Above** The Adoration of the Shepherds at East Harling in Norfolk, painted in the distinctive style of the late fifteenth-century Norwich workshops, has the grainy quality characteristic of wood-block illustration.

engraving, reflecting his own eclectic training and the technical ingenuity of the city in which he lived. In 1496 and again from 1505 to 1507 Dürer spent time in Italy, and his printed works were an important medium for the dissemination of his own ideas and what he had learned of Italian art. His series of woodcuts (*The Apocalypse*, the *Life of the Virgin* and the *Greater and Lesser Passions*) and his engraved works (the *Engraved Passion* and single images such as *Knight, Death and the Devil* and *St Jerome in his Study*) spread his fame far beyond his native city and he attracted numerous pupils. Many of Dürer's own compositions were copied and adapted for stained glass; the 1529 east window of Balliol College, Oxford, for example, draws upon his engraved *Passion* published in 1512.

**Above** Mary of Burgundy, wife of Maximilian Duke of Austria, from the chapel of the Holy Blood in Bruges. Mary is dressed in the steeple hat fashionable in the late fifteenth century, and holds her pet dog in the crook of her arm.

Very little late fifteenth- and early sixteenth-century Netherlandish stained glass survives to complement the panel paintings of the Netherlandish Renaissance. Stained glass was a major casualty of the Calvinist iconoclasm of the later sixteenth century and the southern Low Countries (modern Belgium) suffered losses during the Napoleonic period. The superb donor figures of c.1495 from the Chapel of the Holy Blood in Bruges (removed and sold to an English collector in 1795, and now in the Victoria and Albert Museum) reveal that glass-painters were in the forefront of artistic achievement. The related heraldry from the chapel demonstrates the superb technical mastery of these craftsmen. The heavily restored windows by Arnoult de Nijmegan and Henri de Campes in Tournai Cathedral of c.1500 still convey an impression of splendour, although Arnoult's work is now best admired in Rouen where he worked c.1502–12. The other important scheme of the first half of the sixteenth century is that in Brussels Cathedral, spanning the period c.1520 to c.1550, where the earlier glass is by the Brussels artist Nicholas Rombouts and later glazing by Bernard van Orley, court painter to Margaret of Austria and Mary of Hungary, another artist who had spent time in Italy, where he became familiar with the work of Raphael. Of the work of the flourishing and important sixteenth-century Antwerp glass-painting community very little survives in their native land. However, such was their artistic reputation and entrepreneurial skill that they were employed in Spain, at Granada, Segovia and Salamanca, and in the northern Low Countries at Gouda. The glazing of the church of St Jan at Gouda (in the modern Netherlands) represents the high point of Netherlandish glass-painting. With its large number of surviving cartoons, the glazing scheme offers an unparalleled opportunity to study the relationship beween graphic design and its translation into glass. The scheme spans the turbulent period of Reformation and rebellion that split the north and south Netherlands during the course of the sixteenth century. The principal artists responsible for the glazing were the Gouda glass-painters Dirck and Wouter Crabeth. The earliest window (1555), depicting the Baptism of Christ, was by Dirck and was the gift of the Bishop of Utrecht. Other windows were given by members of the Spanish royal family, for the Low Countries were at that time ruled by Catholic Spain. Dirck's Last Supper window contains donor portraits of King Philip II and his wife, Mary Tudor, eldest daughter of Henry VIII and remembered in English history as 'Bloody Mary'. Another window, also by Dirck, was the gift of Prince William of Orange, who led the rebellion against the king. For a time this window with its donor portrait was blocked up. Two windows were the work of Lambert van Noort (executed by Digman Meynaert) from Antwerp. In 1572 the city of Gouda joined the rebellion and as a result some of its glass was removed by the Calvinists. Fortunately many of the windows were left untouched and the glazing was continued and completed in 1603, under a different political and religious regime (see p. 119). Gouda remains the most extensive and best-preserved monumental glazing scheme in the ancient Low Countries and almost the only substantial stained glass to survive in the north.

One type of glass-painting from the ancient Low Countries that has survived in some quantity, although many examples are no longer in their country of origin, is the silver-stained roundel. Produced largely for the domestic consumer, these exquisite, small-scale panels reveal the technical prowess of Netherlandish painters and prove that when working in this delicate medium the glass-painters were the equals of the panel-painters. Roundels were also popular in cloisters and individual cells in monastic foundations, in situations where they could be an aid to personal devotion. Many of the leading artists of the day designed roundels, including Lucas van Leyden, Pieter Coecke. van Aelst, Dirck Crabeth, Maarten van Heemskerck and Marten de Vos. Their original drawings, some of which survive, were copied for use in the glazier's workshop, and designs were further disseminated as woodcuts or engravings, although, as the market became more competitive and lucrative, artists took steps to protect their designs.

Over two-thirds of the ancient stained glass to survive in France dates from the sixteenth century. This considerable production was achieved in spite of growing political and religious unrest, culminating in the violent wars of religion after 1562. Despite poor survival rates, it is now recognized that Paris was a major glass-painting centre. The most important extant examples are the windows of 1532 and 1533 in St Germain-l'Auxerrois by

**Left** King Philip II of Spain and his queen, Mary of England, donors of Dirck Crabeth's Last Supper window in St Jan's church in Gouda. Another window (see p. 119) contains a portrait of Philip's enemy, William Prince of Orange, who led the rebellion of the Northern Netherlands against Spanish rule.

**Right** The story of beautiful Susanna, wrongly accused of adultery through the perjured testimony of the lecherous elders, was an extremely popular subject for roundels. This example is in the Victoria and Albert Museum, London.

Jean Chastellain, to whom Jean Lafond has attributed the glass at the church of St Aspais at Melun and a window dated 1531 in Bayonne Cathedral. The unusual subject of the Bayonne window, Christ and the Canaanite woman, is depicted in the open air and in its head types reveals the influence of Raphael. To the north of Paris can be found glass attributed to the 'Master of Montmorency', so-called after his most important patrons, the Montmorency family, and particularly Anne de Montmorency, Constable of France and councillor to King Francis I. Montmorency and his family are depicted in glass in the parish church at Ecouen, site of their most important residence, in the collegial church of St Martin at Montmorency and in the chapel of the château of Chantilly, the latter originally installed in the chapel of the château of Ecouen. Forty-four scenes of the loves of Cupid and Psyche, made for Ecouen, are also preserved at Chantilly and abound with delicate Italianate motifs.

In sixteenth-century Rouen stained glass was dominated by two major figures, Arnoult van Nijmegan and Engrand Leprince. Arnoult, who signed his Tournai Cathedral glass 'Arnt Nimegan', also signed two of his Rouen works, the St Stephen scenes now in the church of Saint-Romain, and the Jesse Tree of 1506 in the church of St Godard (where he signs as 'Arnoult de la Poi[nte])'. He introduced a new decorative Renaissance vocabulary to Rouen and was a decisive influence in the formation of styles in Normandy. The Beauvais glass-painter Engrand Leprince furnished glass for the Cathedral of Rouen in 1528 (now lost) and for the church of St Vincent. His Works of Mercy window was made in collaboration with his brother Jean, and the window contains the initials ELP and ILP. The Life of St John the Baptist is dated 1525 and 1526 and bears the initials ALP, ELP and LP. The most celebrated window by Engrand and his brother is probably the Triumph of the Virgin. The window is dated 1515 on the wheels of the chariot and is signed ELP and 'Jehan le Pri...Pri'. It is perhaps on the strength of this window and his famous Jesse Tree for the church of

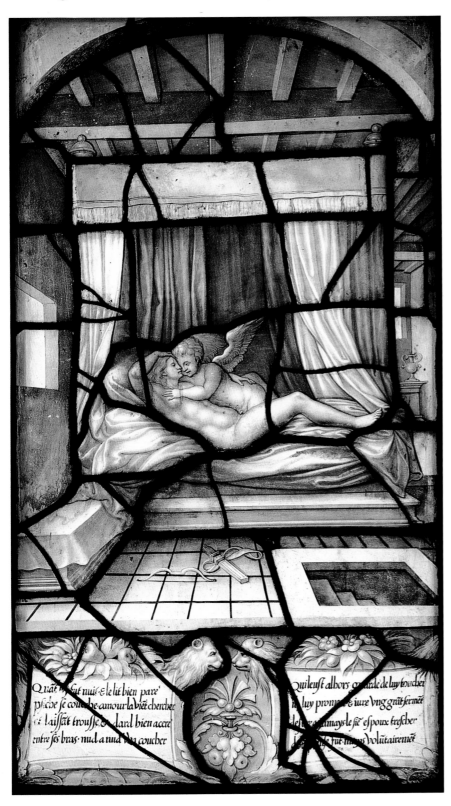

Quāt [...] fut nuit·& le lit bien paré
pſiche ſe cou[...]he amour la viēt chercher
& laiſſāt trouſſe[...] dard bien acere
entre ſes bras· nud a nud [...]la coucher

qui leuſt alhors g[...]de de luy toucher
[...]luy prom[...] iure vng grāt ſerm[...]
de[...] a[...]mays le ſic eſpoux treſcher
[...] fut m[...]ns voluntairem[...]

**Left**  This overtly worldly scene, from the story of Cupid and Psyche, was made for Anne de Montmorency's château of Ecouen.

**Above** St John the Evangelist turns sticks and stones into gold and jewels, from a window by the workshop of Arnoult van Nijmegan, made for the now-demolished church of St Jean in Rouen, now in Wells Cathedral.

St Etienne in Beauvais that Engrand's justifiable celebrity rests. The church of St Vincent was destroyed during the Second World War, but its wonderful glass can now be seen in the exciting setting of the new church of St Joan of Arc in Rouen.

In Lorraine, stained glass was dominated by another artist who signed his work, the Strasbourg-born Valentin Busch. His earliest work in the region was for the church of St Nicholas-de-Port near Nancy. In 1520 he was made official glass-painter to the Cathedral of Metz, a post he held until his death in 1541. Busch was stylistically indebted to German art and in particular to Hans Baldung Grien, an artist whom he may have known personally. The city of Troyes, already cited for its fine twelfth-century glass (see p. 48–9), continued as a major centre of glass-painting activity in the first half of the sixteenth century. Much of the work of the Troyes ateliers lacks originality of content as a result of continual use and reuse of the same designs, demonstrating that a quasi-industrial approach to the production of stained glass is not a phenomenon invented by the Victorians. Other Champagne cities with important stained-glass workshops were Châlons-sur-Marne and Reims.

The history of glass-painting in England has been artifically distorted by the violent break with the past brought about by the Reformation and the Dissolution of the Monasteries. Even without this abrupt dislocation of their working environment, however, native glass-painters were already facing stiff foreign competition for commissions. Imported Flemish and Franco-Flemish manuscripts and painted panels had contributed to the development of a taste for the more pictorially and stylistically advanced paintings produced by Continental artists. Although prolific local workshops continued to make stained glass for local patrons, their work no longer satisfied the more sophisticated tastes of those who had travelled to Europe or who had seen imported works of art originating in Italy, Flanders, Germany or France. A petition of 1474 to Edward IV from the London Glaziers' Guild reveals that by the last quarter of the fifteenth century foreigners were beginning to settle in London in significant numbers. By taking up residence in Southwark, outside the boundary of the city, they managed to elude the guild regulations which applied to their city-based opponents. Richard III then banned the importation of completed windows, but did nothing to curb foreign artists settled in England. It was in fact, the Crown and the circle of the court that accelerated the demise of the native craft. In 1497 the Fleming Barnard Flower was appointed king's glazier to Henry VII, a post he continued to hold under Henry VIII. Flower was authorized to employ three or four other foreign craftsmen. He was no doubt engaged to work on all the most important royal commissions of the early sixteenth century, and it has been argued that he was also involved c.1490–1500 in the glazing of Fairford in Gloucestershire, the only English parish church to preserve a complete medieval glazing scheme. His work at Fairford cannot be substantiated with documents, while his involvement at King's College, Cambridge, can: on 30 November 1515 the sum of £100 was paid to him for glazing at the chapel. By 1517 Flower was dead, and was replaced as king's glazier by another foreigner, Galyon Hone, who together with

Richard Bond, Thomas Reeve and James Nicholson, was commissioned to provide stained glass for the east, the west and sixteen other windows in the chapel. James Nicholson, a Fleming with an anglicized name, was the principal glass-painter employed by Cardinal Wolsey. In 1529 he received £28 for armorial glass for Cardinal College in Oxford, now Christ Church, most of which survives in the hall, and it is his handwriting that has been identified on the Brussels and National Gallery of Scotland *vidimuses*.

Both the Wolsey drawings and the surviving glass in King's College Chapel reveal that it was stained glass in the Renaissance style that prominent patrons now sought, and the expatriate glaziers based at Southwark could furnish this. A string of early sixteenth-century commissions dispersed throughout the country bear the hallmark of the Southwark glaziers and all these commissions were for patrons with connections at court. At West Wickham in Kent, for example, glass of c.1500 in this 'Anglo-Flemish' style is associated with Sir Henry Heydon (d.1504), related to the ill-fated Anne Boleyn. It has been suggested that Roger Ratcliffe, a gentleman of the Queen's Bedchamber to Queen Catherine of Aragon and possibly also to Queen Jane Seymour, may have employed Galyon Hone in 1537 to provide stained glass for the Withcote Chapel in Leicestershire. Queen Catherine and King Henry themselves appear in glass of c.1520 commissioned for the Trinity Chapel of the Chapel of the Holy Ghost in Basingstoke, now in the chapel of the Vyne (Hampshire). The windows were commissioned by Sir William (later Lord) Sandys, Treasurer to the city of Calais. It is possible that Sandys, like Wolsey, employed foreign artists in the preparation of designs, taking advantage of his sojourn in Calais in the royal service.

There is little evidence that the ideas of the Reformers had much impact on sixteenth-century stained glass, although it could be argued that they fostered the spirit of individualism and the importance of personal virtue as a means to salvation. Panels designed for private contemplation and personal devotion, particularly the increasingly popular silver-stained roundels, frequently depicted scenes and stories that urged sobriety, thrift and charity and preached against vanity, gluttony and worldliness. Overtly anticlerical or even Protestant imagery in stained glass is rare; Hans Jacob Kilschperger's satirical panel of a mill for grinding priests (now in the National Museum in Zurich), perhaps a deliberate perversion of the allegorical 'Host Mill' of c.1450 preserved in Berne Minster, is just as unflattering to the Protestant Reformers who feed the Catholic clergy into the hopper.

The Reformation is remembered chiefly as the agency of much destruction and despoliation of stained glass. In England its impact was considerable, while in France, which remained a Catholic country, Protestant rebels destroyed glass along with other so-called 'superstitious' images in the 1562 occupation of Lyons, Le Mans and Poitiers. In the northern Low Countries (now the Netherlands) widespread Calvinist iconoclasm followed the revolt against Spain which began in 1566. Although it continued to be commissioned, even by the Protestant Church – the Gouda glazing scheme was not completed until 1603 – stained glass was about to enter its own dark age.

**Above** The prohet Johel in the Withcote Chapel (Leicestershire), possibly by the King's Glazier, Galyon Hone. The window was made c.1537, on the very eve of the English Reformation. In 1538 Thomas Cromwell, Chancellor to King Henry VIII, issued injunctions against religious imagery.

Tous les cantons de ce large Vniuer
En ont testé par les Euangelistes,
Et les on escrit les pensers
uillant d'icy les anciens pistes

Tous urais Chrestiens le douent receuoir
Auec respect des Prebtres de l'Eglise,
Mais il conuient premierement auoir
l'ame contrible et la coulpe remise

Ce pressoir fut la Venerable croix
Ou le sang fut le Nectar de la Vie
Quel sang celui par qui le roy des Rois

Dans des Vaisseaux en reserue il
Par les docteurs de l'Eglise, pour est
Et sauement de no pe
Mesme de ceux qu'on a Venant, a na

Pape Prelate Prince
ont au celle mis au
le Vin au cœur
Et donte à l'Ame une sain

**Heureux homme Chrestie**    **si fermement tu crois**
**Que dieu pour te sauuer**    **á souffert a la croix,**
**Et que les Sacrements**    **retenus a l'Eglise.**
**De son sang precieux**    **ont eu commencement:**
**Qu'en les bien receuant**    **toute offence est remi**
**Et qu'on ne peut sans eux**    **auoir on sauuement.**
*In te domine speraui non confundar*    *in æternum. psal. 30*
*Non nobis domine non nobis sed nomini*    *tuo da gloriam. psal. 113.*

S E      S E

# THE AGE OF ENAMELS

From the second half of the sixteenth century onwards, religious change and political unrest contributed to a serious disruption of the glass-painter's world, and stained glass continued to decline in popularity throughout the seventeenth and eighteenth centuries. A number of factors were responsible for the low esteem in which the craft was almost universally held. The changing religious climate in those countries affected by the Reformation drastically reduced demand for imagery in churches; in the 1560s the Bishop of Winchester, Robert Horne, ordered the removal of 'crosses, Sensars and such lyke fylthie Stuffe' from the chapel of Trinity College, Oxford. In the seventeenth century England witnessed renewed destruction of 'superstitious imagery' by Protestant divines acting with parliamentary approval. Much of the damage done to windows in Canterbury Cathedral, including the Royal Window in the north transept, dates from Richard Culmer's attacks of 1643, and in 1645 a Protestant news-sheet records the removal of 'the popish pictures and superstitious images' from Cardinal Wolsey's great east window of Hampton Court chapel, which was filled with plain glazing. In late eighteenth-century France, such stained glass was destroyed in the name of 'Revolutionary Reason'.

An equally important contributory factor to the reduced circumstances in which glass-painters worked in the seventeenth and eighteenth centuries was the changing aesthetic climate. Prevailing architectural fashion favoured classicizing styles, in which coloured figurative glass had no place. In 1678 the Celestine monks of Lyons had their stained glass windows removed and replaced with plain glazing, and in a similar spirit between 1789 and 1793

**Above**  The personification of Spring (late sixteenth century), after an engraving by Martin de Vos. Panels of this sort were ideally suited to the domestic interior, where the small-scale detail and delicate colouring could be appreciated.

**Opposite**  Painted in the first quarter of the seventeenth century, this impressive depiction of Christ and the Mystical Wine Press in the church of St Etienne-du-Mont in Paris, was restored in 1734 by the Le Vieil brothers.

James Wyatt removed the vestiges of medieval glazing from Salisbury Cathedral in favour of plain quarries.

Those artists and craftsmen who persevered with the medium of stained glass were also faced by serious technical difficulties. The supply of pot-metal glasses was very limited. In 1636 Louis XIII ordered the destruction of all palaces and castles in rebellious Lorraine, one of the principal centres of glass production, a catastrophe that also affected the glass industry. It is clear, however, that the significance of this single event has been greatly exaggerated, for as pot-metal glass was required for the manufacture of enamel colours, its production cannot have ceased entirely. By 1550, enamel colours were already in use alongside traditional techniques and afforded the glass-painter a range of painterly effects that suited the climate of taste in which he now worked. The drastic decline in demand for coloured window glass was no doubt just as significant in bringing about

**Right**  Hans Wendel Schwerer and his wife commemorated in 1675 by Hans Caspar Gallati of Wil, who has initialled the panel at the bottom. The top of the panel depicts a bath house, with simple bull's-eye glazing in its windows.

a decline in production, although a surprisingly large number of windows executed in enamel stains continued to use significant quantities of pot-metal glasses. Nonetheless, enamel stains came to dominate glass-painting in the seventeenth and eighteenth centuries.

No comprehensive history of enamel glass-painting has yet been written and the picture is thus a partial one. Many writers have denigrated this period of glass-painting, describing it only in terms of decline and poor standards. Recent scholarship, however, has greatly increased the list of glass-painters known to us and has gone some way to redressing the balance. The virtues of this often delicate and meticulous aspect of glass-painting are today far better appreciated. Enamel stains are now recognized as being particularly well-suited to the sort of small panels, roundels, armorials and medallions produced in large numbers in the seventeenth century to fulfil commissions for houses and private chapels.

In Switzerland, where it is thought that enamel stains were first developed, armorial and figurative panels, often of a commemorative nature, were produced in great numbers to satisfy the demands of an increasingly assertive and wealthy middle class. Many of these panels are now found in churches, houses and museum collections outside Switzerland, having been avidly collected by connoisseurs and collectors of the nineteenth and twentieth centuries. The versatility of enamels and their suitability for these small-scale panels led to the virtual abandonment of traditional pot-metal techniques in the making of delicate works of this kind. Designs were provided by some of the leading artists of the day, and relatively large numbers of cartoons, on paper, survive. The names of several glass-painters are known, for many panels are signed; and many are dated, although the date usually refers to the event commemo-rated and may not reflect the point of execution. It is clear that glass-painters were based in numerous Swiss cities – Zurich (Christoph and Josias Muerer and Hans Jakob Nueschler), Berne (Samuel Sybold, Thuring Walther, Hans Jakob Guder and Hans Jakob Dunz), Winterthür (Christ-

**Above** The arms of the Dutch physician Johannes Jansen, dated 1638, surrounded by delicate festoons of foliage ornament. The stylish lady and gentleman at the base would have been copied from a book of engravings.

**Above right** Christ Driving the Moneylenders from the Temple of a late sixteenth-/early seventeenth-century enamelled Swiss roundel, now at Longleat House in Wiltshire.

ophel Kuster, Hans II Jegli, Ulrich Meier, Jakob Weber) and Constance (Jeronymus and Wolfgang Spengler), for example. Small roundels, traditionally painted in glass paint and yellow stain, were now decorated with the full palette of enamel colours. Swiss roundels are filled with incident, the upper half containing a figurative scene and the lower containing intricate armorials and superb lettering, in continuation of the commemorative tradition of the larger, leaded panels. By 1700, however, these attractive coloured panels had been eclipsed by cheaper engraved versions.

Roundels continued to be produced in great numbers in the Low Countries (the Netherlands and Belgium), in response to an unceasing demand for small panels for domestic settings and as a focus for contemplative devotion. Whereas the sixteenth-century roundel was commonly placed in a relatively simple border and set in the upper part of a window against a background of diamond quarries or 'bull's-eyes', the settings of the seventeenth century became increasingly elaborate. The roundel formed the centrepiece of a complex grid of square quarries decorated with cartouches, inscriptions, armorials, swags, arabesques, classical architectural motifs, putti, and charmingly realistic plants, flowers and figures in contemporary dress. These incidental details were taken from the plethora of printed sources now available to glass-painters. Such motifs could also be used to decorate diamond or square panes for simpler quarry glazing schemes, like the one in Lydiard Park in Wiltshire.

The seventeenth century was a period in which Science became part of the education of a gentleman. This is reflected in the popularity of stained-glass sundials, which combined a knowledge of mathematics with a fascination for scientific instruments. A surprising number of stained-glass sundials survive from the seventeenth, and to a lesser extent from the eighteenth centuries, although examples of sixteenth-century date have also been found. The earliest one is probably that in the Kunstgewerbemuseum in Berlin, dated 1535. Glass sundials conform to the same principles as vertical wall dials and each one had to be calculated and made for a particular window. Their combination of decoration and utility assured their popularity. The drilling of the hole to hold the gnomon, the indicator which cast the shadow on the dial face, required considerable skill and numerous dials are embellished with spectacularly realistic painted flies, spiders and even bees, that appear to have alighted on their surface. Over thirty dials survive in England alone.

Surviving seventeenth-century monumental glazing schemes are relatively rare. Some glazing activity continued in the cities of Troyes and Bourges; Bourges Cathedral preserves an impressive window of 1619 given by Gabrielle de Crevant, widow of the Marechal de Montigny, which is based on an engraving by the Italian artist Taddeo Zuccaro. Documentary research by G.M. Leproux has demonstrated that Paris continued to support a significant glass-painting community well into the seventeenth century, tangible evidence for which is preserved in some of its parish churches. The mortuary chapels of St Etienne-du-Mont, constructed in the first decade of the seventeenth century, were provided with seventeen large windows in enamels, while St Eustache preserves eleven windows painted in 1631 by Antoine Soulignac. In both instances, however, these schemes represent the fulfilment of plans laid in an earlier era, for the two churches were begun in the late fifteenth and early sixteenth centuries.

In the northern Low Countries, now known as the Netherlands, widespread religious iconoclasm followed the successful Calvinist rebellion against Spain, drastically affecting the historical appreciation of stained glass. One of the few surviving monumental schemes is that in St Jan's church, Gouda, where, as in Paris, the seventeenth-century windows complete a deferred scheme of an earlier date. In 1573 the church was given over to the Reformed Church and the latest windows reflect the changed religious climate. Of the three post-Reformation windows, one depicts Freedom of Conscience (1596) in an allegorical triumph, and the Biblical relief of Samaria (by Cornelis Cloc, 1601) is paired in a typological manner with the historical relief of Leyden (by Dirck Jansz. Verheyen, 1603), a key incident in Holland's struggle against the Spanish.

**Above** This dial is almost certainly the work of John Oliver (1616–1701), employed to provide glass for the London Weavers' Company in 1669. The panel, minus its gnomon, survived the destruction of the old hall in 1856 and the zeppelin raids of 1916. In the centre a spider advances on a fly.

**Right** Delicate portraits of King Charles I and Queen Henrietta Maria in the Hall of Magdalen College, Oxford, may be the work of Richard Greenbury, employed to glaze the chapel in 1632.

In England, the post-Reformation decline in monumental glass-painting had been particularly serious, perhaps because the craft had already become so reliant on foreign glass-painters. The accession of Charles I in 1625 brought about an important shift in religious policy, for Charles favoured a restoration of liturgical ritual and attempted to reverse some of the changes brought about by the Puritans. In this he was assisted by William Laud, who was made Archbishop of Canterbury in 1633. One aspect of the 'Laudian revival' involved the reordering of church interiors, and in particular the restoration of the liturgical east end, so that emphasis on the sacraments replaced the primacy of the pulpit. At the same time there was a renewed interest in pictorial glass-painting, greatly encouraged by Laud, although his predecesor Archbishop George Abbot had also promoted glass-painters — Holy Trinity church in Guildford, Abbot's home town and site of his famous hospital, contains glass of 1621 by Baptista Sutton. Laud's influence was particularly strong in Oxford University, of which he was chancellor from 1628 and it is in Oxford, which was also experiencing something of a building boom in the early seventeenth century, that enamel glass-painting in England can best be studied. A small number of local glass-painters have been identified, notably Robert Rudland who worked at Wadham, and Richard Greenbury, responsible for the sepia-toned figures in Magdalen College (1632) and probably for the exquisite portraits of Charles I and Henrietta Maria in the oriel of the Great Hall. Two figures are of particular importance in this history: Bernard and Abraham van Linge, glass-painters from Emden in Germany. Bernard, the elder of the brothers, came to England after spending two years in Paris, where his work may have been seen by his first English patron, Nicholas Wadham, founder of Wadham College. Bernard executed the east window of the college chapel, which he signed and dated (1622), working alongside other glaziers, including Rudland and Lewis Dolphin, the second of whom also worked at Hatfield House. Bernard brought with him a familiarity with Continental painting styles and pictorial sources; his Wadham window drew upon engraved book illustrations by Martin de Vos, published in Antwerp in 1595. His only other known work was at Lincoln's Inn (c.1623–6, destroyed during the Second World War) and he had returned to Emden by 1628. His short-lived sojourn in England encouraged his brother Abraham to try his luck abroad, and it is likely that Abraham helped with the Lincoln's Inn commission, through which he received a commission for the St John parish church of Lydiard Tregoze (1627–8) and Lydiard Park (1629) in Wiltshire. He also worked at Hampton Court, Herefordshire (1629), and was probably responsible for the east window of Battersea church (1631). The 1630s were spent providing glass for Oxford colleges; Lincoln (1629–31), Christ Church (1637), Queen's (1635), Balliol (1637) and University (1641). Abraham had become an English citizen and presumably had every intention of remaining in England. However, the outbreak of the Civil War in 1642 cut short his English career and after University College no more is heard of him.

The period of the Commonwealth was a dark one for stained glass in England. Many churches suffered war damage. The detonation of a powder store in Norwich in 1648, for example, blew in all the windows at nearby St Peter Mancroft and destroyed much of its medieval glass. Cathedrals such as Chester, Durham and Winchester were wilfully damaged by soldiers and further injunctions against idolatrous imagery were enacted from 1643 onwards. In Suffolk and parts of Cambridgeshire, the Parliamentary Visitor William Dowsing supervised considerable destruction. Elsewhere the main panels were preserved at the expense of the heads of the saints, which were either defaced or removed. Notwithstanding, a small number of artists continued to work in stained glass, confining themselves to heraldic and non-religious work, and the fortunes of the craft improved with the restoration of Charles II in 1660. Even then Protestant zealots took their

**Above**   The Deposition of Christ from Hampton Court in Herefordshire by Abraham van Linge, dated 1629, is based on Rogier van der Weyden's fifteenth-century picture of the same subject. Abraham's initials have been scratched onto the top rung of the ladder. The panel is now in the Victoria and Albert Museum, London.

**Left**   The relief of Leyden, the most celebrated event in the Dutch war against the Spanish, painted by Dirck Jansz. Verheyen in 1603, includes a portrait of Prince William of Orange, the hero of the Dutch struggle. In the background are the *Watergeuzen* (Sea Beggars), the sea-borne rebels.

**Right** The east window of Wadham College, Oxford, was glazed in 1622 by Bernard van Linge, a glass-painter from Emden in northern Germany. Although the van Linge brothers are remembered as painters in enamels, Bernard has used a significant quantity of pot-metal glass in this window.

toll; in 1679 Prebendary Edward Fowler took it upon himself to break out the west window of the choir of Gloucester Cathedral, which depicted the Trinity, a medieval survivor that had escaped the attentions of even the puritanical Scots, who had damaged much during their occupation.

Little large-scale work survives from the latter part of the seventeenth century, but the artists responsible for it deserve mention for their enterprise and perseverance, if not for their artistic skill. In York, a city which had largely escaped the worst excesses of war thanks to the intervention of Lord Fairfax, the Parliamentary commander and himself a Yorkshireman, Henry Gyles (1645–1709), described by the antiquary Ralph Thoresby as 'the famousest painter of glass perhaps in the world', continued the city's glass-painting traditions, albeit in enamels of variable quality. His work is almost entirely of a secular and heraldic nature, exemplified by his window of 1676 for John Frescheville at Staveley in Derbyshire, probably his finest surviving window. Some of his most effective work is on a small scale, like the sundial at Nun Appleton Hall near York (1670). A second name worthy of note is William Price the elder, who may have learnt the craft from Henry Gyles's father Edmund, and who provided an east window for Christ Church in Oxford in 1696 and the east window of

Merton College (1711–13). William's son Joshua and grandson, also William, followed in his footsteps and were amongst the most talented and technically proficient of the enamel glass-painters.

Joshua Price benefited from his father's Oxford contacts and in c.1717 was awarded the commission for the glazing of Queen's College, where he was required to incorporate glass from the medieval chapel into a new scheme. This was achieved with great sensitivity. Probably his most important commission, however, was for the enormously wealthy Lord Chandos, who entrusted him with the glazing of the chapel at his sumptuous house, Canons, in Edgware near London. When the Canons estate was broken up, the glass was purchased by Lord Foley and reset in Great Witley church in Worcestershire by Joshua's son, William. The Great Witley windows, executed 1719–21, are entirely at home in Great Witley church, consecrated in 1735, where they can be seen together with Lord Chandos' ceiling paintings and stucco decoration, executed by Antonio Bellucci and Pietro Martire Bagutti respectively. Price's bright and delicately coloured windows, painted in an Italianate style from designs by Francisco Slater, are

**Left** The Supper at Emmaus, painted for Lord Chandos' house, Canons, by Joshua Price in 1719–21 and now in Great Witley church, Worcestershire.

**Right** A detail of King George III from William Peckitt's window of Alma Mater presenting Isaac Newton to the king, in the library of Trinity College, Cambridge (1775). The design was prepared by Giovanni Baptista Cipriani.

an integral part of what has been described by Sir Nikolaus Pevsner as 'the most Italian ecclesiastic space in the whole of England'.

Joshua's son William shared his father's sensitivity when working with glass of an earlier era. In his superb windows for the chapel of New College, Oxford (1735–40), he not only incorporated surviving fragments of late fourteenth-century glass, but also designed canopies for his stately figures that imitated the style of the medieval ones. He achieved remarkably rich colours with subtle handling of light and shade and his enamel stains were exceptionally well fired and have suffered little of the pigment loss that so often mars enamel glass-painting.

After Price's death in 1765 the college employed William Peckitt of York to continue the reglazing programme. Peckitt, who was to become the most famous glass-painter of his day, was self-taught and much of his early work is found in York, where he was employed to restore glass in the Minster for his patron, Dean Fountayne. He was a poor draughtsman and his best work is that based on cartoons supplied by others, notably Biagio Rebecca, whose designs were used for his second series of New College windows (1774) and for the south transept window in York Minster (1793). For his 1775 window in the library at Trinity College, Cambridge, the design was supplied by Giovanni Baptista Cipriani.

It appears to have become almost standard practice for the most prestigious commissions to employ designs by the leading painters of the day, a trend which no doubt encouraged the pictorial, illusionistic painting styles which in most cases were so ill-suited to the technique and the medium. In 1723 Sir James Thornhill was paid £100 for sixteen large oil paintings from which Joshua Price was to paint the north rose of Westminster Abbey. The paintings have recently been identified in Chinnor church in Oxfordshire. The dramatic window of Moses and the Brazen Serpent painted in 1781 for Salisbury Cathedral by James Pearson was designed by John Hamilton Mortimer. As superintendent of japanned ware in Matthew Boulton's famous Soho factory in Birmingham, Francis Eginton was accustomed to commissioning designs from painters; Angelica Kauff-man and Benjamin West had both supplied designs for Soho ceramics and Eginton continued this practice when he turned to stained glass. In 1789 he actually hired Benjamin West's painting of the conversion of St Paul so that he could copy it in glass for St Paul's church in Birmingham, and in 1791 he executed a window depicting the Resurrection for the Trinity Chapel of Salisbury Cathedral after a design by Sir Joshua Reynolds, a composition he also supplied to Lichfield Cathedral.

Reynolds is perhaps the most famous eighteenth-century English artist to have worked with glass-painters and took his best-known stained-glass commission, for the west window of New College, Oxford (1775–85), extremely seriously. He prepared a series of full-scale oil paintings from life for the Irish glass-painter Thomas Jervais to work from. Despite Jervais's extremely skilful execution of the work, the window was not a success and Reynolds was bitterly disappointed. The reason for the failure was quickly appreciated by that most shrewd of connoisseurs, Horace Walpole. His response to the Nativity, exhibited in London with artificial illumination, was enthusiastic, describing it as 'glorious' and having 'a magic effect'. However, he quickly recognized that *in situ* the window was too high and that 'Jarvis's colours, being many of them not transparent, could not have the effect of old glass'.

This realization that enamel-painted glass could not achieve the effects of medieval glass resulted in a number of serious academic studies of the history of glass-painting. In 1774 *L'Art de la peinture sur verre et de la viterie* by the Parisian glazier Pierre Le Vieil was published posthumously. In Strasbourg Jean-Adolphe Dannecker lost a fortune made in gingerbread manufacture in his attempts to recover the secrets of the ancient glass-painters. In 1733 John Rowell, a plumber and glass-painter from High Wycombe, offered his clients 'The Antient Art of Staining Glass with all the Colours Reviv'd' and in 1793 William Peckitt wrote a serious treatise entitled 'The Principles of Introduction into that rare but fine and elegant art of painting and staining of glass', which contained recipes for making coloured glass. In particular, he claimed to have rediscovered how to make flashed ruby. The treatise was never published.

Very little French stained glass of eighteenth-century date survives to complement Le Vieil's important contribution to its history. A window of 1756 by the ill-fated Dannecker is preserved in the Musée de l'Oeuvre Notre Dame in Strasbourg and the church of Saint-Roch in Paris has a rather poor window of c.1710 by Guillaume Le Vieil, Pierre's brother. Guilluame was employed at about the same time to glaze the chapel royal at Versailles, where he worked to cartoons supplied by the royal painter de Fontenay. The work was of a decorative rather than a figurative nature, essentially plain glazing with coloured borders. Sens Cathedral preserves a restored Crucifixion of 1748 by an unknown glass-painter. In 1741 and 1753 Pierre was employed to remove medieval glass from the nave and choir of Notre-Dame in Paris, replacing it with similarly plain windows, although his interest in the medieval glass he was displacing prompted the writing of his history. In the closing decade of the eighteenth-century and the early years of the next, stained glass in France was a victim of republican sentiment. In 1792 the Convention National sequestrated the estates of all religious institutions and this was followed in 1796 by a general suppression of religious houses. The effects of this act were felt beyond France's borders, for in 1793 she annexed Belgium and by 1794 had occupied parts of the Rhineland, despoiling many of its churches and monasteries. As in post-Reformation England, religious houses were sold to the highest bidder. Some were then demolished for their building materials (the fate of the great monastery of Cluny), while others were put to secular use. In 1803 the Archives Judiciares were installed in the upper chapel of the Sainte-Chapelle. Two metres at the bottom of each window were blocked to accommodate cupboards to hold the documents and the displaced thirteenth-century glass was used to fill holes higher up the windows, while the rest was sold to a glass-painter. In the same year the buildings of the nunnery of Herckenrode in Belgium were turned into a textile factory and a sugar refinery and its stained glass and works of art were sold off. The beneficiary of much of this despoilation was Alexandre Lenoir (1761–1839), a keen revolutionary but also a devotee of French art. His Musée des Monuments Français, in existence until c.1818, rescued many *objets d'art* and stained-glass windows, although a number of items were severely damaged in the course of their removal to the museum. In 1802 he published a catalogue of his collection, listing the twelfth-century glass from St Denis removed in 1799, and a series of sixteenth-century windows from the Temple church in Paris, one of which has been identified in Southwell Minster in Nottinghamshire.

In 1802 the French Republic made peace with the coalition of European states ranged against her, and for a brief period, before the outbreak of the Napoleonic Wars, travel and trade were once again possible. We have seen how some connoisseurs like Horace Walpole were conscious of the shortcomings of contemporary work in stained glass. Cultured travellers abroad in Europe immediately after the Peace of Amiens had no trouble in purchasing medieval and Renaissance masterpieces in stained glass for as little as the price of some plain glazing to replace the discarded treasures. Three hundred and forty panels from Herckenrode, for example, were purchased in 1803 by Sir Brooke Boothby, who immediately upon his return to England sold them for £200 to the Dean and Chapter of Lichfield Cathedral, where they can be seen today. John Christopher Hampp, a German by birth, travelled widely in his capacity as master weaver and merchant of Norwich, where he had settled in the 1780s, and in addition to his textile transactions, he acquired large quantities of glass in Paris, Normandy (particularly Rouen), Aachen, Cologne and Nuremberg. In 1804 the collection amassed on these trips was offered for sale at Hampp's Norwich warehouse and at Mr Christie's auction house in Pall Mall. A number of major private collections of medieval glass were formed in England in the opening years of the nineteenth century and Englishmen were among the first to develop an interest in the works of the Middle Ages. At Costessey Hall in Norfolk, Lord Jerningham built a Gothick chapel for his manor house and filled it with medieval glass. In Essex, Sir Thomas

**Above** Derided by contemporaries, the exceptional quality of Thomas Jervais' execution of Joshua Reynolds' cartoons for the west window of New College, Oxford, is revealed by close scrutiny.

Neave formed a similar collection at Dagenham Park, and at Strawberry Hill Horace Walpole created possibly the most famous collection of all. All these have since been dispersed and many of their choicest pieces have found their way into museum collections in every part of the world. In Germany, the poet Goethe filled his house in Weimar with examples of all of the many things that interested him and his collection included a number of panels of medieval glass. A German collector on a larger scale, whose career in some respects parallels that of Hampp, was Christian Geerling, a Cologne wine merchant. In 1827 he exhibited a large number of items salvaged from the secularized churches of Cologne, and many of them are now in German museum collections.

Collecting medieval glass, although a pastime confined to a relatively small number of men with antiquarian tastes, was important in creating an intellectual climate in which medieval stained glass was valued rather than derided. While James Wyatt was supervising the removal of the thirteenth-century grisaille of Salisbury Cathedral, a vigorous campaign against him was waged by certain readers of *The Gentleman's Magazine*. Glass-painters like William Price, who installed glass for Walpole, and Betton and Evans of Shrewsbury, employed to install the Herkenrode panels at Lichfield, gained valuable experience in handling medieval glass. The increasing sympathetic study of medieval windows and a growing appreciation of their technical superiority provided a fertile ground for the ensuing Gothic revival in stained glass.

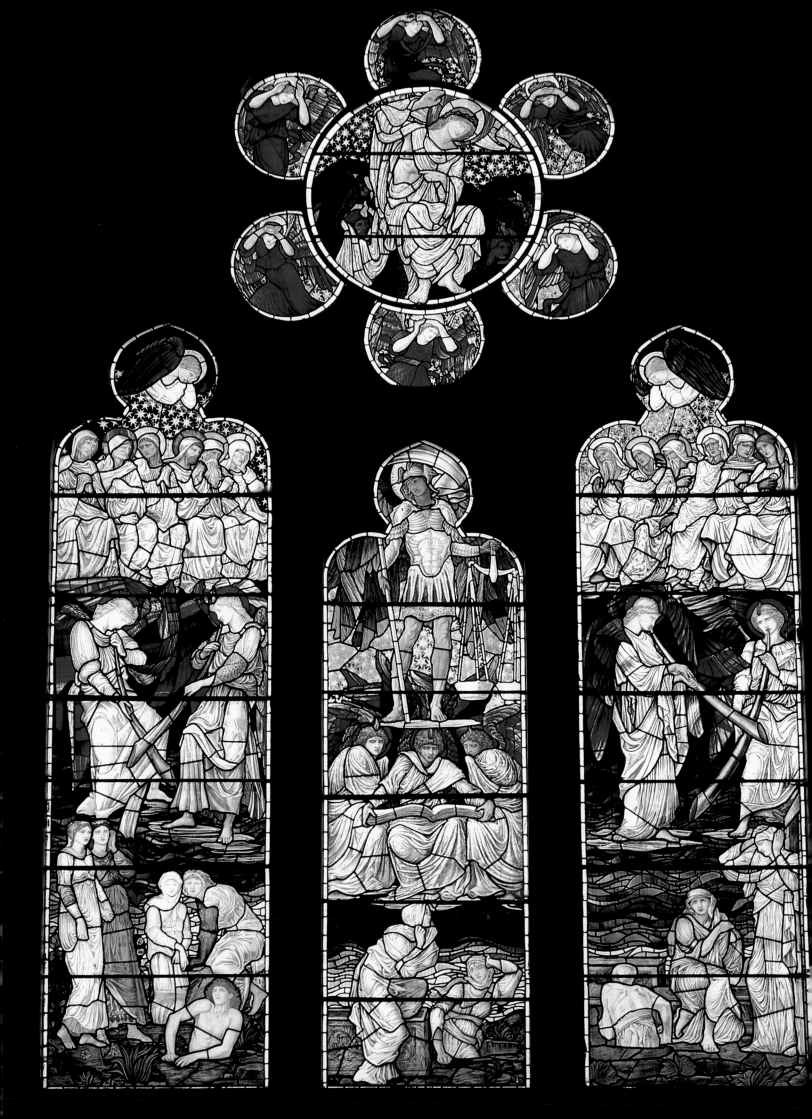

# FROM GOTHIC REVIVAL TO ARTS AND CRAFTS

The early years of the nineteenth century witnessed what Sir Nikolaus Pevsner has described as 'the fancy dress ball of architecture'. Classical, Gothic, Italianate and even 'Hindoo' styles all had their champions in architectural circles. While every style found its supporters when it came to the design of country houses, railway stations and public buildings, in the design of new churches the Gothic style emerged as the most popular with architect and patron alike. In a revival of stained glass it was also Gothic that was to provide the most appropriate model, offering both a stylistic example and a technical tradition. By the middle of the eighteenth century connoisseurs, of whom Horace Walpole was one of the most influential, had appreciated the shortcomings of contemporary enamel glass-painting in comparison to the medieval glass the collectors were beginning to prize. Throughout Europe, and in England in particular, a dissatisfaction with the products of an industrial age led artists to revere the crafts of pre-industrial times. In Germany the Nazarenes expressed this ideal in paintings that combined a Catholic sentiment with a Renaissance style. In England from the late 1840s the Pre-Raphaelite Brotherhood represented the same romantic, historicist ideals.

Religious and political factors were propitious for the Gothic Revival. In 1772 Goethe wrote his influential essay 'Von Deutscher Baukunst', in which he identified Gothic as the German national expression, while in England in the 1830s the architect and designer A.W.N. Pugin (1812–52) described Gothic as the true Christian style, associating Classicism with paganism. Of all the European countries, it was England that embraced Gothic with the

**Above**  In trying to translate Ford Madox Brown's painterly style into stained glass, the craftsmen of Morris, Marshall, Faulkner & Co. have used enamel stains as well as pot-metal glasses. This window, made in 1870, is at Meole Brace in Shropshire.

**Opposite**  The Last Judgment, Easthampstead (Berkshire), designed by Edward Burne-Jones in 1876, in his mature Italianate style.

greatest fervour. In 1835 the Ecclesiastical Commissioners embarked upon a plan of extensive church building in response to the enormous development in new urban centres ill-served by existing churches. Between 1840 and 1900 they averaged 100 new churches per year. The emancipation of Roman Catholics in 1829 and the restoration of a Catholic ecclesiastical structure in England in 1852 generated further demand for new churches; and Catholics like Pugin, who had travelled in Europe, had been impressed by the richness of Catholic art on the Continent, denied them in England by the usurpation of the Reformation. Thomas Rickman's 1819 classification of the Gothic style provided the style debate with a vocabulary. Pugin, a convert to Catholicism since 1835, was a formidable apologist for Gothic. His *True Principles of Pointed or Christian Architecture* (1841) and *An Apology for the Revival of Christian Architecture in England* (1843) were models of

**Right** Painted in 1825, Johann Friedrich Overbeck's Madonna and Child clearly reveals its debt to the painters of the Italian Renaissance.

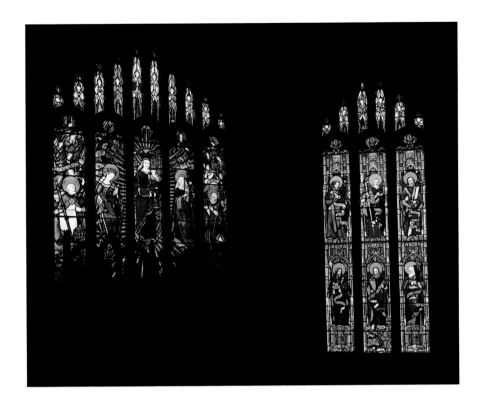

**Left**  For his windows in the Roman Catholic college chapel at Oscott, in Warwickshire (1838), Pugin employed the little-known William Warrington. By 1842 this partnership had ended, as the exacting Pugin sought a more sympathetic craftsman to execute his designs.

erudition. His views were ably supported by the journal of the Cambridge Camden Society. *The Ecclesiologist*, published between 1841 and 1868, was instrumental in shaping opinion in both architecture and the decorative arts, although it was the organ of a society closely allied to the Oxford Movement, which sought the regeneration of the Anglican Church. Its spiritual base may have been somewhat different from Pugin's, but its influence was to have much the same effect. In 1847 Charles Winston had provided students of stained glass with a stylistic framework akin to Rickman's for architectural styles in his book *An Inquiry into the Difference of Style Observable in Ancient Glass Paintings*, an analysis unsurpassed today.

Pugin's first stained-glass commission, for the Roman Catholic college of St Mary, Oscott, Warwickshire, was by no means the first new glass to be executed in a Gothic style. Thomas Willement made his first window, of a purely heraldic nature, in 1812, and by 1830 was producing figurative works in a medieval idiom. Betton and Evans were capable of creating superb windows in a medieval style and undertook a number of important restorations of medieval windows (most notably at Winchester College and St Lawrence, Ludlow). In Newcastle, William Wailes gave up his grocery business in 1835 and turned to stained glass. William Warrington had been a pupil of Willement and was the author of *The History of Stained Glass*, published in 1848. It was he who executed Pugin's Oscott designs.

None of these artists could match Pugin in the creation of archaeologic-ally accurate medieval designs. His travels had given him a wide experience of medieval stained glass and his understanding of the medium was considerable. He favoured the figure and canopy formula of the fourteenth century, and in his two windows for the Bartley family in St Mary the Virgin, Oxford, he eschewed a slavish copying of medieval models and dressed his donor figures in contemporary dress. The earlier of the two windows was executed by William Wailes. The second was made by the studio of John Hardman of Birmingham, who, like Pugin, was a Roman Catholic. In 1838 he had established an ecclesiastical metalworks and in 1845 was encouraged by Pugin to take up stained glass. Pugin was chief designer for the firm until his death in 1852.

The 1850s saw the emergence of a new generation of Gothic Revival architects and of a second formative influence, the art critic John Ruskin (1819–1900), whose interest lay not so much in architectural form, but in architectural decoration and in particular in the use of colour in architecture. Stained glass was accorded an important place in the polychrome interior and the 'High Victorian' architects had pronounced views on the role of

**Right**  Installed at Davington Priory in Kent, the artist's own home, this panel by Thomas Willement reveals his exceptional talent as a heraldic glass-painter. Willement was a renowned scholar, heraldic artist to King George IV and stained-glass artist to Queen Victoria.

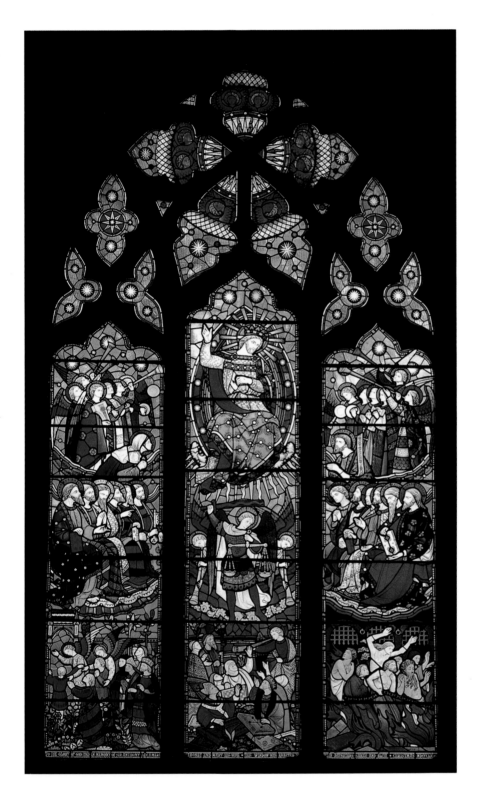

stained glass and the proper relationship between architect and glass-painter. Although the older firms continued to win commissions, new firms were also founded, in response to the burgeoning demand for stained glass. William Butterfield (1841–1900), one of the hardest taskmasters where stained glass was concerned, quarrelled with John Hardman Powell, Hardman's new designer. For his windows in the chapel at Keble College, Oxford (1873–4), and for the west window of All Saints, Margaret Street, in

**Above**  Robert Turnhill Bayne had been trained by Clayton and Bell, but from 1862 became a partner and chief designer for the new firm of Heaton, Butler and Bayne, one of the most original of the Gothic Revival firms. This window at Friday Bridge (Cambridgeshire) was made in 1866.

**Opposite above**  The work of the French firm of A.N. Didron, seen here at Feltwell in Norfolk (1859), was meticulously and archaeologically faithful to its thirteenth-century models.

London (1877), he employed the more malleable Alexander Gibbs. The architectural work of G.E. Street (1824–81) fell increasingly under the influence of French Gothic and he began to use the new firm of Clayton and Bell, whose designs, under Street's supervision, began to draw on French thirteenth-century models. The firm was responsible for training a number of prominent stained-glass artists of the later nineteenth century, including C.E. Kempe, John Burlison and Thomas Grylls, and became one of the most technically proficient and prolific of the Victorian companies. From 1859 Clayton and Bell collaborated briefly with Heaton and Butler, which from 1862 became Heaton, Butler and Bayne. By the end of the 1860s Heaton, Butler and Bayne had proved to be one of the most imaginative of the trade firms. Their early windows show the stylistic influence of Clayton and Bell, but they were later to be more strongly affected by the styles of the more inventive artists, especially Henry Holiday, whose works they began to execute. Stained glass was now designed in a far wider variety of styles than the fourteenth-century style advocated by Pugin. While the sixteenth century had some supporters (including Charles Winston), the styles of the twelfth and thirteenth centuries, especially the great French cathedral series, were to be the models most often emulated.

The cultural, religious and political conditions prevailing in France in the early decades of the nineteenth century were rather different. During the Revolutionary and Napoleonic periods, a great deal of stained glass had been destroyed and dispersed. The restoration of the monarchy under Louis Philippe was to be of critical importance in a stained-glass revival. The Orleanist monarchy sought to enhance its reputation and underline its legitimacy by identifying with its medieval Capetian forebears. The glazing of the royal chapels at Carheil (1842–8) and Dreux (1843–4) by the Sèvres factory was executed in enamels, using cartoons supplied by artists like Delacroix and Ingres. The king and his family took a personal interest in the scheme, which mixes universal and French royal saints. The figure of St Ferdinand at Dreux has the features of the Duke of Orleans, while the cartoon for the figure of St Philip, used at both Carheil and Dreux, has the physiognomy of the king himself.

In France, as in England, the experience gained in the handling of medieval glass during restoration was of great importance in establishing stylistic and technical principles. In April 1816 Alexandre Lenoir's Musée des Monuments Français was dissolved and where possible its art treasures, many of them severely damaged or defaced, were returned to their original locations, a process taking several years to effect. In 1818 the St Denis windows finally returned to the abbey, and, from 1816 to 1846 under François Debret and from 1847 to 1879 under Viollet-le-Duc, attempts were made to restore them. In 1839 the collaboration of the architect J.B. Lassus, the antiquary Adolphe Napoléon Didron, the designer Louis Charles Steinheil and the chemist Reboilleau, resulted in the creation of the Passion window installed in St Germain-L'Auxerrois, tangible proof that contemporary craftsmen and designers could achieve the standards of the medieval past. A.N. Didron founded the Didron stained-glass atelier and in 1844 the *Annales Archaéologiques*, an important vehicle for the dissemina-

tion of information and discussion on medieval topics. His book on medieval iconography, *Iconographie Chrétienne, histoire de Dieu*, was published in 1843, and appeared in English translation in 1851, complementing Mrs Jameson's *Sacred and Legendary Art* of 1848.

In 1847 the École des Beaux-Arts in Paris held a competition to find the artist best qualified to be entrusted with the restoration of the windows of the Sainte Chapelle. The winner was the young Henri Gérente. Didron had described his window of the Life of the Virgin for Notre Dame de la Couture in Le Mans (1844) as the finest he had ever seen. His early works had been made by a variety of studios, but from 1844 he ran his own atelier and fulfilled a large number of commissions. His knowledge of iconography and his craftsmanship were unparalleled in France at this time and his familiarity with medieval styles was based on close study of original medieval glass, including fragments in his own collection. He had also undertaken a number of restorations, notably at Lyons Cathedral. He died in 1849 at the age of only 36, and the Sainte-Chapelle commission passed to the runner-up in the 1847 competition, Antoine Lusson of Le Mans, who had executed

**Above** The Duke of Orleans was the model for this figure in enamels of St Ferdinand in the royal chapel at Dreux (1846) by the Sèvres factory. The cartoons for the twelve figures of saints were supplied by the painter Ingres, while Viollet-le-Duc provided the architectural canopies and borders.

Gérente's Le Mans window so admired by Didron. The Gérente atelier was continued by Henri's brother Alfred, who formed a close association with the architect Eugène-Emmanuel Viollet-le-Duc (1814–79), the most prolific and influential figure in French archaeological restoration. By 1870, the increased demand for stained glass in France resulted in the same tendency to industrial mass production so typical of the English trade firms. Between 1837 and 1867 the workshop of Maréchal de Metz alone is thought to have produced 12,000 windows.

As in France, so in Germany the intervention of the Crown was of great importance in fostering the revival of stained glass. Ludwig I of Bavaria was an enthusiast for the art of the Middle Ages and northern Renaissance, collecting paintings of this period for the new Munich Museum (now the Alte Pinakothek). The Middle Ages were identified as the greatest period of German religious, artistic and political achievement, with Dürer revered as its greatest genius, although in stained-glass circles the style of Peter Hemmel von Andlau was widely copied. At the Royal Bavarian Glass Painting Manufactory, founded by the king in 1827, Sigismond Frank undertook technical experiments to improve the quality of enamel colours.

In Germany it was the styles of the late Middle Ages and early Renaissance that were particularly favoured by glass-painters, in contrast to the majority of English and French artists, who, in the period up to c.1860, were drawn to the art of thirteenth and fourteenth centuries. This no doubt reflects the powerful influence of the Nazarene school of painting. Johann Friedrich Overbeck (1789–1869), its most important figure, founded a Brotherhood of St Luke, named after the patron saint of many medieval painters' guilds, which in 1810 settled in a monastery just outside Rome. The work of the Nazarenes was characterized by a religious idealism combined with a style derived from that of Dürer, Raphael and Perugino. Their influence was also felt in England, for from the 1840s many of their paintings were available as prints. A number of Overbeck's painting were actually translated into stained glass. In the work of Charles Clutterbuck and George Hedgeland the Nazarenes had their English imitators, in spite of the disapproval of pictorialism expressed by *The Ecclesiologist*.

Heinrich Hess, a member of the Nazarene school, was made artistic manager of the Royal Bavarian Manufactory, and carried their strongly pictorial style into the most important centre of German stained-glass production. The west wall of Regensburg Cathedral was glazed under Hess's direction (1826–9), while at Au, on the outskirts of Munich, a scheme of nineteen windows in a late fifteenth-century style was paid for by the king (1834–43). Engraved folios of these windows popularized the work of the Bavarian Manufactory, whose works were exported throughout Europe and to America.

By 1860, stained glass had experienced a substantial revival throughout Europe. In England, in particular, it had been restored to a position of prominence in the decorative arts and the craft had become dominated by a stylistic historicism, in which the champions of the thirteenth, fourteenth, fifteenth and sixteenth centuries argued for the particular virtues of their preferred style. Thanks to the experimentation of Charles Winston in

**Above** Lithographs of the windows at Au near Munich helped to popularize the work of the Royal Bavarian Manufactory in Europe and America. Using superb enamels, these delicate and refined works found favour with those who favoured a more pictorial style. The influence of the fifteenth-century windows of Peter Hemmel is shown in the canopies (see p. 17).

England and Alexandre Brongniart in France, glass-painters were able to use a range of pot-metal glasses that approached in quality and texture the materials of the Middle Ages. However, success now threatened the medium with creative infertility as the most prolific commercial firms turned to quasi-industrial mass production in order to meet the massive demand for their products.

It was against this industrialization of the applied arts that William Morris (1834–96) wrote and campaigned so effectively. Together with John Ruskin, he was to be one of the most influential figures in nineteenth-century cultural life, and the effect of his ideas about art, literature and political thought was considerable, extending far beyond the shores of England and the century in which he lived. In the history of stained glass William Morris is the most important figure of the second half of the nineteenth century, and in the stained glass of Morris and his circle a truly original expression developed, an idiom that rejected a slavish, archaeological imitation of Gothic and fuelled an enormously creative phase in the history of English stained glass.

Morris and Edward Burne-Jones (1833–98) had met as undergraduates at Oxford, where both had come under the seductive influence of the Oxford Movement. Both had considered a career in the Church, but disillusionment led instead to art, which they embraced with as much romantic idealism and fervour as they had religion before it. On graduating, Morris went into the Oxford office of the architect G.E. Street, and Burne-Jones, intent upon becoming a painter, went to London to seek out Dante Gabriel Rossetti (1828–82), one of the founder-members of the Pre-Raphaelite Brotherhood. Under Rossetti's influence, Morris too took

**Left**   In the small watercolour, the *Tune of the Seven Towers* of 1857, Rossetti's fascination with the opulence and romance of the Middle Ages is expressed in a cramped, illogical space, typical of his compositions.

**Above**   The Red House at Bexley Heath (1859–60), designed for William Morris by Philip Webb.

up painting, a decision that altered his course decisively in favour of the decorative arts. The group of young artists that gathered around Rossetti were strongly infected by his obsession with the Middle Ages. 'Medievalism was our *beau idéal*', wrote the painter Val Prinsep.

Morris was a wealthy man, and after his marriage to Jane Burden he commissioned a house from the architect Philip Webb which was to epitomize in its architecture and decoration all that the group valued in art and craft. The collaboration of Morris and his friends in the decoration and furnishing of the Red House at Bexley Heath (1859–60) was formative in the establishment in 1861 of the firm of Morris, Marshall, Faulkner and Company (re-established as Morris and Company from 1874–5). The partners' declared aim was the regeneration of the decorative and applied arts according to medieval ideals of craftsmanship. From the beginning, stained glass was an important aspect of the firm's work, and in the early years, Morris, Burne-Jones, Rossetti, Webb and Ford Madox-Brown all provided designs for glass. Rossetti's interest in the medium was relatively short-lived, dating from the period 1861–4. His penchant for crowded, small-scale scenes was not well suited to stained glass, although some of his compositions, notably the Sacrifice of Isaac at Peterborough Cathedral, were exceptionally effective. Ford Madox Brown (1821–93) supplied over 130 designs to the company, containing mostly the smaller-scale aspects of the firm's commissions. Philip Webb (1831–1915) was responsible for the overall design of some of the firm's earliest and most successful windows, and also supplied a large number of designs for borders, canopies and the beautiful tile-like quarries that are so distinctive an aspect of the company's work of the 1860s. As an architect, his approach to the management of space within a window was architectural. Empty or awkward spaces were often filled with canopy work, a solution abandoned in the later windows, in which Morris increasingly substituted foliage forms for architectural frames.

Morris himself produced a number of stained-glass compositions, not all of them completely successful. His most important contribution lay in the overall co-ordination of the execution of the windows, the design of backgrounds and the choice of colour and texture. The influence of his work in textile and wallpaper design is immediately evident. Morris and Company windows, largely as a result of Morris' intervention, were typified by a subtlety of colouring that set them apart from the work of contemporary rivals. This contribution to the company's stained glass was

**Left**  St Augustine and St Catherine designed by William Morris for the east window of Middleton Cheney, Northamptonshire (1865), in which the foliage background beloved by Morris appears in one of Morris, Marshall, Faulkner & Co.'s finest windows.

most significant in Morris' collaborations with Edward Burne-Jones, who after 1874–5 became the firm's principal designer. Burne-Jones' greatest interest lay in his paintings and so his stained-glass cartoons, in which his superb draughtsmanship is immediately apparent, were supplied uncoloured. It was at this point that Morris and the team of skilled craftsmen and glass-painters employed by Morris and Company took over, realizing the design in stained glass.

Burne-Jones' talent as a designer of stained glass had already been revealed in his earliest works, executed before the creation of Morris, Marshall, Faulkner and Company. One of his undoubted masterpieces in the medium is the St Frideswide window in Christ Church Cathedral, Oxford (1859). In its breaking-up of space into small, crowded compartments, the influence of Rossetti is apparent. The window is filled with incident, each panel containing large numbers of figures, executed in rich, sparkling colour. The figures are naturally posed and each scene fills the full width of the light. A medieval atmosphere is created by costume and incidental detail, rather than by the application of a rigid Puginesque Gothic setting. The window was executed by James Powell and Sons, the firm responsible for Burne-Jones' impressive, if rather confusing, rose window and Jesse window for the restored Waltham Abbey (1861).

In the course of the 1860s and 1870s, Burne-Jones as a painter became less and less the imitator of Rossetti and more and more the admirer of the Italian masters of the Renaissance. As classical mythology came to occupy a prominent position in the subjects of his paintings, so the sculptural, monumental grace derived from a study of fifteenth-century masters like Botticelli transformed his painting style. This sculptural quality was enhanced by the treatment of the tightly creased classical drapery of his figures. The transformation is evident in two of his most famous works in glass of the 1870s, the Vyner Memorial (1872) and the St Cecilia window commemorating Edith Lidell (1875), both in Christ Church, Oxford, and in the dramatic Last Judgment at Easthampstead, Berkshire, of 1876. The Oxford windows can be seen alongside the earlier St Frideswide window, demonstrating very effectively the stylistic evolution of a decade. The classically draped figures in the later windows are pale and sculptural, set off against cool foliage. Small scenes beneath each of the main-light figures serve as predellas in the manner of Italian panel paintings.

The 1870s were the decade in which Victorian architects and designers embraced a wider range of stylistic sources, resulting in an imaginative eclecticism which has been christened the 'Aesthetic Movement'. In architectural circles this was manifest in a revitalization of domestic and vernacular styles – English, Dutch and even Japanese. English architects and designers were no longer in thrall to ideals of national identity or religious propriety as they had been in the 1840s. Many stained-glass firms adhered to Gothic styles, but under the influence of freelance designers such as Henry Holiday (1837–1927), Harry Ellis Wooldridge (1845–1917) and the Swede Carl Almquist (1848–1924), companies like James Powell and Sons and Shrigley and Hunt produced windows in the Aesthetic idiom. In a more conservative mould, one of the older firms to adopt a new range of stylistic

**Above** Cartoon for an angel for the St Catherine window at Christ Church Cathedral, Oxford (1877–8), by Edward Burne-Jones.

**Left** St Frideswide hides from her pursuers in a pigsty in the St Frideswide window in Christ Church Cathedral, Oxford (1859), by Edward Burne-Jones. In its crowded composition and strong colour, the window reveals Rossetti's influence on the young Burne-Jones.

models was Burlison and Grylls. Both John Burlison and Thomas Grylls had trained with Clayton and Bell, and yet much of their finest work was in a fifteenth-century or early Renaissance style, drawing on the work of Dürer and his circle for inspiration. Another prolific firm responsible for an enormous number of windows that made good use of the rich and decorative nature of fifteenth- and early sixteenth-century art was the firm of C.E. Kempe, founded in 1869.

Unlike many of the designers of his day, Henry Holiday took a considerable personal interest in the execution of his own designs for stained glass. He designed for Powells from 1863 until 1890, although one of his finest schemes, that for Worcester College, Oxford, was executed by

Lavers and Barraud. The Worcester College windows reflect his interest in the art of the Classical world, and his solemn, monumental figures are an essential part of William Burges' classical and Etruscan redecoration of the chapel interior. Holiday also painted the frieze beneath the windows, in which he was assisted by Wooldridge. A trip to Italy in 1867 introduced Holiday to the art of Giotto and the Italian trecento and in his 1869 apse window for G.E. Street's St Mary Magdelene, Paddington, classical and Renaissance influences mingle in one of his most successful commissions, executed by Heaton, Butler and Bayne. Holiday's reputation outside England was considerable, and a number of his windows were exported to America. In 1890 he visited the United States in person and received a number of extremely important commissions, including seven windows for Grace Church, Utica, a scheme which Holiday himself particularly valued, and the Robert E. Lee Memorial window, for St Paul's church, Richmond, Virginia (with a slightly later version of the design in Durham Cathedral). In this dramatic and exotic window he put to good use his study of Egyptian costume and artefacts. On the strength of these commissions, Holiday acted upon his growing dissatisfaction with Powells, and in January 1891 established his own studio in Hampstead. Holiday, unlike Burne-Jones, had long taken an interest in the materials used to make his windows. In the Hampstead studio he initiated experimentation which resulted in the manufacture of a thick slab glass offering a wider range of colours and textures. On his trip to America he had seen and been impressed by the 'Favrile' glasses of Tiffany and the opalescent glasses of La Farge, and 'HH slab' was his answer to this.

Both Ruskin and Morris had idealized the concept of the artist-craftsman of the Middle Ages and Renaissance. Even so, Morris and Company's glass had been executed in the manner typical of most of the larger trade firms, that is, by the devolution of each of the individual stages of manufacture. The cartoons supplied by Burne-Jones were interpreted in glass by a team of skilled glass-painters. While this arrangement suited Burne-Jones, who had little desire to involve himself in the process, it was less than satisfactory for those designers and painters who wished to be personally involved in the translation of a design into glass and who interested themselves in the material itself. This dissatisfaction was not, of course, confined to stained-glass designers alone. Those artists who developed the ideas of Morris into the tenets of the Arts and Crafts Movement believed in the concept of the 'art-work', the object designed and made, or at least directly supervised in the making, by the artist himself. Artists, designers and architects sharing these ideals banded together in 'guilds', consciously using the terminology of the craft associations of the Middle Ages. The first of these, of brief but influential duration, was the Century Guild of Artists founded in 1882 by A.H. Mackmurdo. This was followed by the broader-based Art Workers Guild of 1884 and the Arts and Crafts Exhibition Society of 1888, whose members included Morris, Burne-Jones, W.R. Lethaby, J.D. Sedding, William de Morgan, Selwyn Image and Christopher Whall. Although Selwyn Image was one of the first designers to apply the Arts and Crafts principle to his stained glass, it was Christopher Whall who was to emerge as the most

**Above**   The archangel Gabriel, by Burlison and Grylls (Moccas, Herefordshire, c.1870), is based on a Martin Schöngauer engraving. Late medieval German art became increasingly influential in the designs of this interesting firm.

**Opposite**   Working for G.E. Street at St Mary Magdalene, Paddington, Henry Holiday produced some of his most successful windows. He later quarrelled with Street over the setting of his designs for Salisbury Cathedral.

**Right** One of Selwyn Image's small number of works in stained glass, made for a private house in Mortehoe in Deven (1881).

important exponent and teacher of its philosophy in the medium. He summarized this in his book *Stained Glass Work*, published in 1905 as part of W.R. Lethaby's *Artistic Crafts Series of Technical Handbooks*. In advising a student on the setting up of his own business, he wrote 'I care not whether a man calls himself Brown, or Brown and Co., or, co-operating with others works under the style of Brown, Jones or Robinson, so long as he observe four things.

(1) Not to direct what he cannot practise;

(2) To make masters of apprentices, or aim at making them;

(3) To keep his hand of mastery over the whole work personally at all stages; and

(4) To be prepared sometimes to make sacrifices of profit for the sake of the Art, should the interests of the two clash.'

Whall's life as a stained-glass artist was an example of this philosophy in action. His greatest scheme of windows was for the Lady Chapel of Gloucester Cathedral (glazed between 1899 and 1909), in which profit was certainly put aside in the interests of achieving Art. The windows are filled with deeply saturated colour set off by areas of silvery white glass. Paint, applied in a gritty, textured manner, was used to control and manipulate the passage of light through the glass. Whall believed that each piece of glass should be 'cared for' and 'nursed' by the glass-painter in order to make the most of its qualities. The naturalism of his figures stems from his practice of drawing from life, unheard of in the trade firms, while the natural world supplied the inspiration for endlessly inventive decorative motifs for collars, hems, brooches, diadems, often resembling Celtic interlace. Figures are framed by 'canopies' of intertwining foliage stems. Backgrounds are made up of a network of irregularly shaped quarries of varied thickness and tone.

Remember Mary Beckett of Somerby day of February 1915 at whose cost

in this Parish who died on the 21st this Church was restored 1882–1884

**Left**   Christ the Good Shepherd at Corringham (Lincolnshire) by Christopher Whall, made in 1914, is typical of Whall's excellent draughtsmanship, mastery of paint and jewel-like Norman slab glass, a difficult material to cut and lead.

**Above** Harmony in colour was one of Christopher Whall's principal aims, beautifully achieved in the Peveril Turnbull Memorial window of 1905 at Ashbourne in Derbyshire, depicting St Cecilia, patron saint of musicians.

**Below** Stages in the manufacture of a bottle using 'Early English' or 'Norman' slab glass. Diagrams by Peter D Cormack.

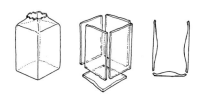

A critical event in the development of Whall's distinctive style was the development in 1889 of a new type of glass by the firm of Britten and Gilson, called 'Prior's Early English Slab' after the Arts and Crafts architect E.S. Prior. This thick slab glass, of uneven thickness and rich colour, made in bottle-shaped moulds (see p. 144), provided Whall and his pupils with a material which was to transform their work. In an article in the *Art Journal* of 1896 it was described as having 'somewhat the effect that cutting gives a gem and is exceedingly brilliant and at the same time cannot be seen through'. This colour could only be appreciated when mixed with pure white glass, and Whall applied the analogy of music to the mixing and balancing of colour: 'Harmony in colour depends not only upon the arranging of right colours together, but the arranging of the right quantities and the right degrees of them together'. In achieving this balance, white glass played an indispensable part.

In addition to fulfilling his own commissions, Whall was a dedicated and influential teacher, taking classes at both the Royal College of Art and the Central School of Arts and Crafts. One of the most talented of his pupils was Mary Lowndes (1857–1929), who in 1897 went into partnership with Alfred John Lowndes, formerly of Britten and Gilson. Lowndes and Drury provided workshop facilities to stained-glass artists, enabling them to execute their work in an Arts and Crafts environment. Whall used the studio, as did Henry Holiday, who provided a link between the circle of Burne-Jones and Morris and the younger artists of the Arts and Crafts Movement. In 1906 Lowndes and Drury moved into a purpose-designed stained-glass studio, the Glass House in Fulham. Edward Woore (1880–1960), who as a student provided illustrations for *Stained Glass Work*, later managed the Whall studio with Whall's daughter Veronica. His later independent commissions were executed in a simpler, less decorative manner, reliant upon strong draughtsmanship and rich colour. Karl Parsons (1884–1934), the second student illustrator of Whall's book, executed a large number of commissions, several of them for export to Commonwealth countries, including South Africa and New Zealand. His best work is characterized by a judicious use of aciding, perhaps influenced by his friendship with the slightly younger Dublin artist Harry Clarke. Hugh Arnold (1872–1915), another Whall pupil, produced a number of fine windows before his early death in the First World War.

Whall's influence was not confined to his own circle of pupils. In Birmingham the young Henry Payne (1868–1940) joined the staff of the Birmingham School of Art in 1889. During the 1890s he was increasingly involved in the designing of stained glass and in 1900 was sent to Lowndes and Drury to receive instruction from Christopher Whall. On his return to Birmingham, he set up a fully equipped studio to execute the designs of his students. The Birmingham School of Art was to produce a number of exceptional stained-glass artists, notably Walter and Florence Camm and Richard Stubington, who replaced Payne as teacher of stained glass at Birmingham after his retirement to the Cotswolds to concentrate on his own work in 1909.

In Ireland the Celtic Revival reformer Edward Martyn, co-founder of the

Irish National Theatre and close associate of W.B. Yeats, began a campaign to revive Irish stained glass. In 1901 Martyn had approached Whall with a view to his setting up a stained-glass school in Dublin. In the event pressure of work prevented this, and Whall sent Alfred Ernest Child (1875–1939), his 'favourite pupil'. Child became the first stained-glass teacher at Dublin's Metropolitan School of Art, and with Whall's help and with the financial assistance of the painter Sarah Purser the co-operative studio workshop An Túr Gloine (The Tower of Glass) was established in 1903. Child trained a new generation of exciting stained-glass artists, taught in the Arts and Crafts tradition, but conscious of their Irish heritage. Michael Healy (1873–1941), Ethel Rhind (c.1879–1952), Wilhemina Geddes (1887–1955) and Harry Clarke (1889–1931) were all to be students at the Dublin School of Art, and all but Clarke, who took over his father's business, made their windows at An Túr Gloine, modelled closely on Lowndes and Drury. All used Irish subjects and themes in their work – Geddes in her Fate of the Children of Lir and Clarke in his choice of scenes from modern Irish literature for his 'Geneva Window'. In 1925 Wilhemina Geddes moved to London where her

**Below** Harry Clarke's Geneva Window of 1929 was commissioned by the government of the Irish Republic to represent the nation at the International Labour Organization in Geneva. The controversial nature of some of its scenes meant that it was never installed.

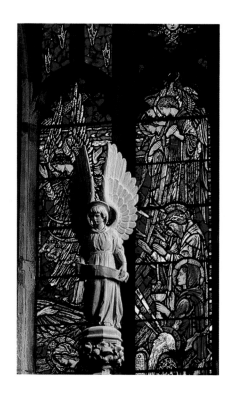

**Above** In the 1928 east window of All Saints church, Porthcawl (Wales), one of his largest commissions, Karl Parsons achieved the flowing brilliance he strove for after his visit to Chartres in July 1924. Parsons was also increasingly influence by his friend Harry Clarke (see p. 145).

**Below** Adam and Eve from a window in the chapel of Lipótmezó Hospital, Budapest, Hungary (1913), designed by Sandor Nagy and made in the workshop of Miksa Róth.

work was made at the Glass House. In London, she was to teach another Irish artist, Evie Hone (1894–1955). Thus the philosophy of Christopher Whall and the Arts and Crafts Movement continued to exert a strong influence well into the present century.

In England and Ireland the Arts and Crafts Movement was strongly wedded to the ideal of uniting design and execution of the art-work – the first of Christopher Whall's precepts. In Europe, artists were less obsessed with the rejection of industrial production, the hallmark of the English movement. This is perhaps explained by the fact that elsewhere the production of the decorative and applied arts had been less thoroughly industrialized than in England. In Europe the concept of *Gesamtkunstwerk*, the totality of harmonious design achieved by the collaboration of a number of artists and craftsmen, was the overriding ideal; this and truth to materials. The European movement was also perhaps less stylistically eclectic; in countries with an emerging sense of national identity, like Hungary and the Scandinavian countries, the artists of the Arts and Crafts Movement drew upon what were perceived to be the traditions of the national and ethnic cultural heritage, rather as An Túr Gloine looked to the Irish past. Arts and Crafts became the vehicle for a Romantic Nationalism.

This rather different emphasis is seen in the stained-glass work of Hungary. By the early years of the twentieth century, the writings of Morris and Ruskin were well known throughout Europe. In 1905 the Hungarian artist Aladár Köröfői Kriesch (1863–1920) published *On Ruskin and the Pre-Raphaelites*, in which space was devoted to a consideration of Morris' stained glass. In 1904 Kriesch together with Sándor Nagy (1869–1950) had founded the artists' Colony at Gödöllő near Budapest. Concentrating initially on textiles, especially carpet-weaving, the community gradually diversified to include leatherwork, ceramics, embroidery and stained glass in their repertoire. The Gödöllő community was also influenced by the social theories of Morris and Tolstoy and aimed to achieve social reform as well as artistic revitalization. Nagy, the most talented designer of glass, worked closely with the craftsman Miksa Róth (1865–1944), who executed his best work. Although Nagy's style was influenced by the art of the English Pre-Raphaelites, best seen in some of his smaller, domestic panels, his subjects originated in Hungarian legend and folklore and like Kriesch he also drew upon folk art. Other motifs can be traced to the circle of the Viennese Sezession. In the 1913 decoration of the Palace of Culture at Marosvásárhely in Transylvania (now Tirgu Mureş in Rumania), the Gödöllő artists achieved real *Gesamtkunstwerk*, with mosaics by Kriesch and Nagy and stained glass in the Hall of Mirrors designed by Nagy and the architect Ede Thoroczkai Wigand (1870–1945), a follower of the architect Ödön Lechner, pioneer of a Hungarian architectural style. The triptych windows depict scenes from the legends of Attila the Hun, a hero of the Magyar past, and Transylvanian folk ballads. The Gödöllő community declined drastically with the coming of the First World War.

In the first half of the nineteenth century, very little indigenous stained glass was made in America. Wealthy patrons imported glass from all the major European studios, and the choice of Munich, Oudinot or Clayton and

Bell came to reflect the religious and political divisions in American society. As a result, the first phase of the American Gothic Revival in stained glass is a mirror image of the European experience. An important home-grown figure in the history of American stained glass is William Jay Bolton, born in England of an American father, who trained at the National Academy of Design in New York. Bolton completed a surprisingly large body of work in a brief career, notably the fifty windows for the church of St Ann and the Holy Trinity, Brooklyn (1844–8). In 1848 he returned to England, where he executed a small number of windows, and in 1854 he entered Holy Orders.

In the windows of Louis Comfort Tiffany (1848–1933) and John La Farge (1835–1910), America made a considerable contribution to Art Nouveau (see Ch. 9), and the products of this 'American School' existed alongside the continued importation of European Neo-Gothic stained glass. By the early years of the twentieth century, however, a reaction against opalescent stained glass had set in and America's twentieth-century Gothic Revival began. The most influential figure in this movement was the architect Ralph Adams Cram (1963–1942), perhaps best-known for the Cathedral of St John the Divine in Manhattan, the largest Gothic church in the world. In glazing the Cathedral, Cram commissioned glass from English firms, notably James Powell and Sons of Whitefriars and John Hardman's but also employed the American stained-glass artist Charles Jay Connick (1875–1945). In Connick, Cram had encountered a fellow spirit; author of the aptly named *Adventures in Light and Colour* (1937), Connick became one of the most influential apologists for this belated Gothic Revival. He repudiated the opalescent glasses of Tiffany and La Farge, using only the mouth-blown antiques of traditional glass-painting. In his working methods, if not his style, Connick was influenced by English Arts and Crafts ideals; members of his studio were trained to be proficient in every aspect of the craft of stained glass. While some of his larger commissions, the Cathedral of St John the Divine (c.1935), for example, look uninspired, his earlier windows at Proctor Hall at Princeton University (c.1919), clearly indebted to the work of Morris and his circle, have a liveliness and decorative richness. Much of his work, however, seems anachronistic and derivative compared to those artists he most admired, including the Irish artist Wilhemina Geddes.

Connick was perhaps one of the most prolific and influential of a new generation of American artists working in a broadly Gothic idiom. William Willet (1867–1921) had trained with John La Farge, but as a result of a trip to Europe and a brief partnership with Connick, became a stained-glass Gothicist, based in Philadelphia. In Boston, the firm of Reynolds, Francis and Rohnstock produced windows strongly influenced by thirteenth-century France. The short-lived Wright Goddhue (1905–31) produced impressive windows for thirty churches before his tragic suicide. Recognizing an important commercial opportunity, the British-born artists J. Gordon Guthrie (1874–1961) and Henry Wynd Young (d. 1923) established a partnership in the United States. Working on a smaller scale, in styles influenced by the late Middle Ages, but with a strong Arts and Crafts flavour, Guthrie and Young were responsible for some of the most effective American glass of the early twentieth century.

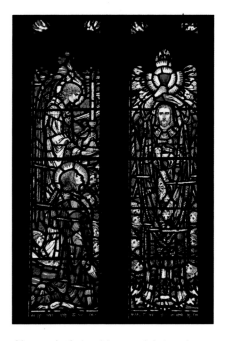

**Above**  In their subjects and their style, Charles Connick's windows for Proctor Hall, Princeton University (1919), combine the influences of William Morris, the English Arts and Crafts Movement and the Middle Ages.

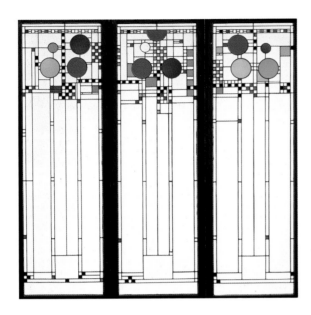

# STAINED GLASS IN THE TWENTIETH CENTURY

The diversity and variety found in stained glass of the twentieth century defy easy definition and classification. The new century began with a widespread desire to formulate new modes of expression unencumbered by the artistic vocabulary of the past. In most European countries, groups of artists reacted against the artistic establishment of the day and this was to be particularly significant for the decorative and applied arts, generally excluded from the embrace of most of the existing fine art academies and salons. In Vienna in 1897, for example, a group of dissatisfied artists and designers founded the Vienna Sezession, an artists' association that stood in opposition to the conservative Wiener Kunstlerhaus, while in England, as we have seen, a series of craft guilds were established.

The world of nature was to provide a fruitful source of new forms and motifs, free of associations with an academic artistic past. Sweeping, curving forms reminiscent of plant stems, leaves and flowers are central to the work of architects, designers and painters who have been branded Art Nouveau after the influential gallery of interior design, the Maison de l'Art Nouveau, which opened in Paris in 1896. Architects and interior designers, like Hector Guimard in France and Victor Horta in Belgium, integrated stained glass into their buildings, in doorcases, skylights and screens, but their glass was generally unpainted and decorative rather than figurative.

One of the leading exponents of European Art Nouveau was the Glasgow architect Charles Rennie Mackintosh (1868–1928). In his design of houses like Hill House, Helensburgh (1903–4), he followed the *Gesamtkunstwerk* ideal of design totality, designing furniture, carpets and glass as

**Above**  In his 1912 windows for the Avery Coonley playhouse (a kindergarten run by Mrs Coonley) in the Coonley residence at Riverside, Illinois, Frank Lloyd Wright anticipated the work of Mondrian and De Stijl.

**Opposite**  Despite his involvement in a number of abstract commissions, Patrick Reyntiens maintains his deep commitment to the painterly, figurative tradition, exemplified by *Harlequin and Pantalon*, one of a commedia dell'arte series from 1989–90.

**Right** Charles Rennie Mackintosh's Willow Tea Rooms in Glasgow's Sauchiehall Street (1904) display the architect's commitment to the ideals of design totality; every aspect of the decoration was architect-designed.

well as the structure. His Willow Tea Rooms in Sauchiehall Street in Glasgow (1904) made extensive use of glass panels (produced by the firm of J. & W. Guthrie), which employed a variety of sinuous and geometric motifs. Mackintosh's work was well known in Europe, and in 1902 he was visited by admiring members of what was to become the Wiener Werkstätte.

France had energetically embraced Art Nouveau and in the work of the Nancy school created works that employed an adventurous range of techniques and new materials, including the opalescent glasses developed in America. The leading figure in Nancy was Jacques Gruber, an artist who drew upon the natural world for inspiration, while being strongly influenced by Japanese art, a combination that gives his work a clarity and an unfussy quality. His intense interest in his materials is clear; although many of the glasses he used were machine-made, he also experimented with the layered techniques used in tablewares by Emile Gallé. The delicacy of his leading is quite exceptional. In Catalonia, Art Nouveau of great flamboyance and individuality is associated with the names of Antonio Gaudi (1852–1926) and Domenechi I. Montaner (1850–1923). Domenech's glass ceiling for the Palau de la Musica Catalana in Barcelona is an architectural *tour de force*, while Gaudi's crypt windows for the chapel of the Güell palace in Barcelona recall early Romanesque windows in their simplicity. Jozef Mehoffer's windows for Fribourg Cathedral (1896–1930s) combine elements of pure Art Nouveau with a strong figure style reminiscent of some of the work of the Hungarian Arts and Crafts artists, while his later designs (for the choir) became increasingly Expressionist in their sweeping, angular forms. The Czech-born artist Alphonse Mucha (1860–1939), best known for his graphic work, also designed for glass. His stunning window for Prague Cathedral, although late (1931), looks like an Art Nouveau poster in glass.

With the popularity of both Art Nouveau and Arts and Crafts interiors, the early twentieth century saw an enormous increase in demand for decorative glass in the domestic context. Private houses, restaurants, hotels, all used glass as part of their interior decoration. Since it was based on engraving, etching and simple leaded-light techniques, much of the glass cannot be said to be 'stained glass', however, and the Church remained the

**Left** The Charles Duncan and William Hegardt Memorial Window (*c.*1924), in Pilgrim Congregational church, Duluth, Minnesota, by Tiffany Studios. The landscape windows were always the most successful, using the qualities of the Tiffany glasses to greatest effect.

**Right** *Welcome* by John La Farge, made in 1909 for number 9, East 68th Street, the New York home of Mrs George T. Bliss.

most important patron, a patron whose significance the domestic and secular market could not hope to usurp. A few significant commissions for churches conceived in a more progressive style were forthcoming. In Vienna, Koloman Moser (1868–1918), a founder-member of the Wiener Werkstätte (Vienna Workshops), established in 1903 with the advice of Mackintosh, designed some very powerful figurative windows, indebted neither to the Gothic past nor a folk art tradition, for St Leopold's church, Steinhof, near Vienna, designed by the Sezession architect Otto Wagner; while in England W.R. Lethaby's All Saints, Brockhampton (Herefordshire), with its concrete vault, was glazed by Christopher Whall. Nonetheless, the majority of stained-glass commissions continued to be for churches built in the Gothic style, either medieval buildings or Gothic Revival buildings, and

Gothic continued to be favoured by many ecclesiastical architects and patrons. This has presented stained glass of the twentieth century with an aesthetic dilemma, and the story has been one of a search for an appropriate new voice and a continuing struggle to demonstrate the contribution that stained glass can make to a range of architectural contexts other than its traditional ecclesiastical one. In the 1990s, stained glass is beginning to have an impact in shopping centres, airports and public spaces. In the 1900s it was still very much a religious art form and that relationship with the Church, which had made stained glass a major architectural art form throughout the Middle Ages, has for much of the twentieth century threatened it with marginalization.

The experience of Tiffany Studios illustrates very clearly the contradictory forces besetting the early twentieth-century designer of stained glass. in the 1893 Columbia Exposition in Chicago, Louis Comfort Tiffany (1848–1933) exhibited a range of domestic and ecclesiastical windows alongside his

**Left** The Russell Sage Memorial Window in First Presbyterian church, Far Rockaway, Long Island, commissioned c.1905 by the widow of a wealthy railway magnate and philanthropist. Tiffany's disregard for the architectural style of the window tracery incensed his critics, including the church's architect, Ralph Adams Cram.

deservedly renowned table glass. His windows were widely acclaimed for their amazing range of new glasses, also used for his tablewares, and in 1900 his work received European exposure at the first Paris Exposition Universelle. Tiffany, who had spent time training in Paris, was an accomplished landscape painter and so was drawn to the natural world as a source of design for his stained glass, an enterprise very close to his heart and one which he continued to promote throughout his career, often in the face of considerable criticism. The Tiffany style, using the superb colours and textures of the 'Favrile' glass made at the Corona glassworks, often plated in double thicknesses, relies on a mosaic effect in which the leadline provides the necessary draughtsmanship and painted detail is used very sparingly. A textured glass for use in draperies was specially formulated to reduce further the need for paint. Tiffany windows are at their most successful when depicting landscape, fruits, flowers, birds and animals. In these windows, with their dreamy, romantic quality, Tiffany's mastery of colour is shown at its best. In handling the large groups of figures necessary for the depiction of Biblical scenes, however, the studio's efforts were far less successful and were handicapped by a lack of traditional iconographical training. In this respect, the work of Tiffany's one-time friend and soon to be eclipsed rival, John La Farge (1835–1910), was altogether more successful. La Farge used a similar range of glasses and a limited amount of painted detail, yet created figurative designs of great sensitivity.

Realizing the weaknesses of his figural windows, Tiffany battled to gain acceptance for his 'landscape' windows in churches, while continuing to produce smaller decorative panels for private houses, clubs and public buildings. An important milestone was the Galbraith Ward Memorial window in the Saint James Episcopal church at 71st Street and Madison Avenue, in New York. In designing windows for churches, attempts were made to select flowers that had religious symbolism – lilies and vines were popular. His more daring (and the largest) of the landscape windows was the Russell Sage Memorial window of 1910 for the First Presbyterian church, Far Rockaway, Long Island, a pictorial landscape glimpsed through the branches of an enormous tree. The window was a popular success, although it was loathed by the architect of the church, Ralph Adams Cram, who thought it irreligious.

Elsewhere, architects and designers now recognized as precursors of the modern movement experimented with more geometric and angular forms. In America Louis Sullivan (1856–1924), Frank Lloyd Wright (1867–1959) and architects of the Prairie School were seeking an indigenous American style. Wright, its leading exponent, designed a relatively small number of extraordinary houses for wealthy patrons, many of them in the Midwest where the pull of the historical past and its visual heritage was less strong. His houses were characterized by interior spaces that flowed into one another to provide comfort, convenience and privacy in a new way. The architecture was regarded as 'organic' in that its planes and outlines were designed to sit comfortably in its landscape. Ornamentalism on the exterior was almost totally eschewed. Every aspect of the interior was designed by the architect, and Wright favoured built-in furniture as a means of making

TO TH
IN THA
LIFE OI
VILLE
WHEL
B.OCT

**Left** Figures of Hope and angels, in a detail from Wilhemina Geddes' Joseph of Arimathea window of 1933 for the Wheler family church at Otterden Park in Kent.

the most effective use of space. Windows and internal screens were filled with panels of unpainted leaded glass, often in stylized versions of natural forms – wheatsheaves, grasses, trees. Large amounts of light or clear glass were used, to allow adequate illumination of the domestic interior.

In England, designers trained in the Arts and Crafts tradition continued to create stained glass of originality and strength that fitted comfortably into a predominantly Gothic idiom. Experimentation in abstract forms can be seen in a very small number of windows made by the Omega workshops, better known for their fabrics, pottery and paintings. Of those that survive one of the most effective is the landscape designed by Jock Turnbull in 1914 (now

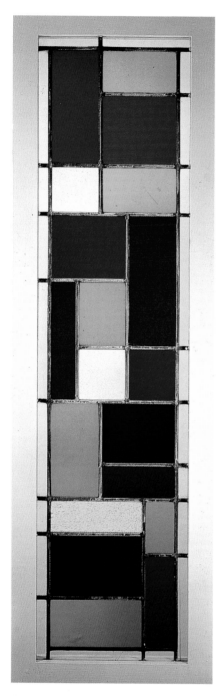

**Above** This door panel, designed by Theo van Doesburg, was executed in 1920 by the department of stained glass at the Weimar Bauhaus.

in the Victoria and Albert Museum), based on a painting by Cézanne. The window relies on the leaded outline and the texture and variations in colour of the glass itself. An even more remarkable early abstract window, conceived on a much larger scale, is the east window of St Mary's church, Slough (Buckinghamshire), of 1915, by Alfred Wolmark.

The First World War generated an enormous demand for war memorial windows, and although many of the trade firms continued to produce designs in a Gothic style, artists such as Karl Parsons, Edward Woore and Wilhemina Geddes created some of their finest work in response to this demand. Geddes became increasingly Expressionist in her later work, although she was always a painter of glass and never turned her back on the use of the painted line to modify colour and light. Her work stands out in British stained glass of the inter-war period as the most strikingly modern in style. Great promise is suggested in a panel preserved in the Victoria and Albert Museum depicting a dramatic figure of St Michael (1928) by the short-lived Frank Barber (1903–32). An artist who relied almost entirely on the mosaic potential of his materials, reserving paint for hands and faces, was Leonard Walker (1877–1964). Walker was influenced by the Arts and Crafts Movement, whose stylistic influence can be seen in his approach to the handling of paint and in the decorative motifs used, for example, in his war memorial window for St Lawrence's church, Brondesbury (c.1918). In his later work, such as his ten windows for the Hong Kong and Shanghai Bank in Singapore, the mosaic effect is more pronounced, although Walker's designs remained strongly figural.

Experimentation with colour and outline is characteristic of the work of the Hungarian designer Józef Rippl-Rónai (1861–1927). Better known as a member of the Nabis group of painters, Rippl-Rónai carried the 'cloisonné' principle derived from Gauguin into a small number of stained-glass commissions, notably the glass ceiling for the Andrassy Palace in Budapest (1898). In his panel for the Ernst Museum in Budapest (1912), the stylized women have been reduced to blobs of colour, the figures turned into areas of pattern. A similar quality is found in Károly Kernstock's designs for the windows for the Schiffer villa (c.1911), with an interior decorated by a number of artists, including Rippl-Rónai. Kernstock (1873–1940) was founder of a group of painters and intellectuals calling themselves 'The Eight' (Nyolcak), strongly influenced by the art of Cézanne and the Fauves. This influence is evident in his monumental *Seven Chieftains* window, in which the figures have a broken-up, modular feel. The strong thick outlines to each mass make the design very effective as a stained-glass design. The work of these two artists was very unlike the more painterly work of Nagy and the Gödöllő artists.

It was in inter-war Germany under the Weimar Republic that stained glass made its greatest advances towards an authentically modern expression. The most original work originated in the circle of the influential Bauhaus, founded in 1919 by Walter Gropius. The stated aim of the Bauhaus was remarkably similar to that of the earlier Arts and Crafts Movement: 'The complete building is the final aim of the visual arts. Their noblest function was once the decoration of buildings. Today they exist in isolation, from which they can be rescued only through the conscious co-operative effort of all craftsmen' (*The First Proclamation of the Weimar Bauhaus*, 1919). The Bauhaus designed for the new building materials of the twentieth century, making use of extensive areas of glass, which could now be machine-made in large clear sheets. Influenced by the theories of the artists of the De Stijl movement, which originated in Holland in the years after the First World War, the glass designed by the Bauhaus is characterized by strong parallel and vertical lines and large expanses of primary colour reminiscent of the paintings of Mondrian. The influence of De Stijl was a direct one, for Theo van Doesburg (1883–1931), editor of the magazine from which the group took its name, was lecturer at the Bauhaus and himself designed stained glass. Van Doesburg was an admirer of the work of Frank Lloyd Wright, whose playroom windows for the Avery Coonley House (1912) have the quality of a Mondrian painting. The Bauhaus at Dessau was closed in 1933 by the Nazis and much of its stained-glass work, including Josef Albers screen-like window for Gropius's Sommerfeld House in Berlin (1921) and Sophie Tauber-Arp's 1926 window for a restaurant in Strasbourg, was destroyed in the Second World War. What has survived is now almost entirely confined to museums and private collections, but reveals that the design principles of the Bauhaus and De Stijl had provided a convincingly modern vocabulary for stained glass.

The dissolution of the Bauhaus and the exile of its artists and teachers (it was re-established in Chicago in 1937) disrupted its practical influence on stained-glass design in Germany. A figure of perhaps greater importance in

**Left** Josef Albers' *Window in Red*, made at the Bauhaus in 1923.

157

**Above** An untitled panel made in 1926 for the Gesolei Cultural Centre in Düsseldorf. This piece, with its strong Art Deco feel, is typical of the jazz-influenced panels designed by Johan Thorn Prikker in the 1920s.

**Right** *Orange*, designed by Thorn Prikker in 1931, represents the last phase of his work in glass, in which he moved ever close to true abstraction. All his later panels were made by Hein Derix Studios, Kevalaer in Germany.

the development of German design in stained glass in the twentieth century has been the outherwise little-known Dutch-born artist Johann Thorn Prikker (1868–1932). Thorn Prikker worked in both an Expressionist figurative and an abstract style. Much of his work has been lost, but in his figurative windows, Hagen Railway station for example, his work is not unlike that of Geddes in his monumentalism and handling of paint, revealing his debt to the German Expressionists of the Blaue Reiter group. His later work became more strictly geometrical in feel, although jazz and Art Deco were probably as important to this evolution as De Stijl. His most remarkable surviving window is also one of his latest: dating from 1931, the year of his death, *Orange* relies on coloured glass of extraordinary intensity and subtlety of tone, arranged in horizontal zones. In this panel, now in the Kaiser Wilhelm Museum in Krefeld, Thorn Prikker anticipates many of the trends found in post-war German stained glass. In his capacity as a teacher, he provided a direct link between the Germany of the 1920s and 1930s and the post-war reconstruction.

· Although German stained glass has continued to offer a place to figurative work, it has been in the development of an abstract idiom that it has had the

**Left** St Thomas, designed in 1958 by Anton Wendling for Propsteikirche, St Maria Himmelfahrt, Julich (Germany).

**Below** One of a series of windows made for Wiesbaden Town Hall by Ludwig Schaffrath.

greatest influence. In the work of Heinrich Campendonk (1889–1957) and Anton Wendling (1891–1965), the abstract and the figurative traditions coexisted and the careers of both artists spanned the dislocation of the Second World War. Wartime destruction swept away much stained glass but also provided enormous opportunities for the post-war generation, making Germany in the 1950s and 1960s one of the most prolific and influential of creative nations in stained glass. George Meistermann (b.1911) began working in stained glass in the 1930s, when Thorn Prikker was a formative influence. His best-known and most influential works date from the post-war period, however, and his work has successfully combined the abstract and figurative, using restless and sinuous forms alongside more structured geometric passages. This 'suggestive' realism is exemplified by his windows depicting Noah's Ark and the Flood in the Marienkirche at Koln-Kalk (1965), while his windows on the *Colour Tones of Music* for the German Radio Station at Cologne (1952) and his *Bottrop Spiral* of 1958 have been recognized as major abstract works. As professor at Aachen Technical School, Wendling trained Ludwig Schaffrath (b.1924), one of the most important post-war designers for glass. Initially influenced by Meistermann, Schaffrath, who has also worked extensively in mosaic, quickly evolved his own distinctive voice. His earliest work is austerely geometric and linear. In his cloister windows for Aachen Cathedral, he relied entirely on line, using no paint and completely colourless glass. Colour has played a more prominent part in his later designs, in which carefully controlled acid

**Above** Noah's Ark by Georg Meistermann in the Marienkirche, Koln-Kalk, executed in 1965 by the Dr H. Oidtmann Studio, is typical of Meistermann's 'suggestive realism'.

**Above right** Installed in the library of the London Hospital in 1990, this window by Johannes Schreiter continues to investigate themes of medical science and technology first explored in his 1977 designs for the church of the Heiliggheist in Heidelberg.

etching produces tonal gradations of great delicacy, while more sinuous lines and figurative hints have become more marked in his most recent work. The use of highly polished lenses is another distinctive feature of Schaffrath's designs, giving his windows a sparkling, sculptural feel. It has been Schaffrath who has done much to promote the use of stained glass in large public buildings.

Johannes Schreiter (b.1930) is possibly the most uncompromising of the post-war German designers, moving away from the use of lead purely for constructional purposes. Stray leads, applied to the surface of the glass, wander across his windows, creating a restless calligraphy against large areas of completely unpainted glass. His work is widely sought by collectors and it is not surprising to learn that a number of his autonomous panels have been inspired by the paintings of Mark Rothko. His iconography is derived directly from the images of the twentieth century: computer print-outs, microchips and molecular structures have all featured in his designs. The German school has been enormously influential in the development of post-war stained glass, particularly in America.

In France stained-glass artists were relatively slow to address the questions posed by Cubism, Expressionism, and Abstraction, and the most dramatic new works date from the period after the Second World War. It has been the participation in stained-glass design of mainstream artists that has contributed to the re-establishment of stained glass as a major, monumental art form. Matisse, Chagall, Braque, Rouault, Cocteau, all names well-known in the story of twentieth-century painting, have designed for glass, the success of their windows relying heavily on their close collaboration with master glass-craftsmen.

Although France had suffered terrible losses during the First World War, most of the war memorial works commissioned in the period after 1918 were traditional and unadventurous in style. An honourable exception is the work of Georges Desvallières, which has the massive, monumental quality found in the work of Hone, Geddes and Thorn Prikker. In 1919 Maurice

**Above** Georges Braque (1882–1963) is remembered as one of the pioneers of Cubism, developed in partnership with Picasso. His particular contribution to Cubist painting was the introduction of typography, a feature of this Jesse Tree of 1955, made for the parish church of St Dominique, Varangeville, the village near Dieppe where he spent all his summers.

**Left** Georges Rouault had served an apprenticeship as a stained-glass craftsman, and his understanding of the medium, his appreciation of medieval art and his own religiosity are all evident in this *Christ of the Passion* (executed by Paul Bony) made in 1948 for the church of Notre-Dame-de-Tout-Grâce at Assy.

**Above** *Flagellation*, one of a series of *dalle de verre* windows designed for the church of the Sacred Heart in Audincourt from 1950 to 1952 by Fernand Léger, executed by Louis Barillet.

**Opposite left** The Tribe of Asher, one of twelve windows designed in 1962 by Marc Chagall (executed by Charles Marcq) for the synagogue of the Hadasseh Medical Centre in Jerusalem.

**Opposite right** Jean Cocteau's hypnotic design *Rencontres du visible et de l'invisible*, executed by the Oidtmann Studio, was made for the Chapelle des Simples, at Milly-la-Forêt, the village where Cocteau (1889–1963) spent his later life, Cocteau is better known as a painter, writer, film-maker and theatrical designer.

Denis had established the Atelier d'Art Sacré in an attempt to rejuvenate religious art, but this was to have only a limited impact and the Church continued to favour traditional styles.

The 1939 Petit Palais exhibition of decorative arts in Paris, which included stained glass designed by Georges Rouault, suggested a new direction. Using deep, rich colours, Rouault imbued his work with a deeply felt spirituality and painted with a heavy outline which translated into glass and lead with ease. The coming of the war was effectively to postpone any fulfilment of this promise. During the war, most important medieval glass was removed for safety and so survived. The same could not be said for nineteenth-century glass, whichs remained *in situ* and suffered accordingly. In the post-war period, therefore, reconstruction offered new opportunities for architects and stained-glass artists alike. That architects thought in terms of commissioning stained glass at all owes a great deal to the influence of the journal *Art Sacré*, run by two Dominican fathers, Marie-Alain Couturier and Raymond Regauney. Under their direction, the journal argued for a greater creativity and freedom in art for the Church, reflecting and participating in the contemporary artistic milieu. Father Couturier was involved in the commissioning of glass to fill the church of Notre-Dame-de-Toute-Grâce at Assy (Haute Savoie), turning the church into a showcase for new French glass. Rouault designed five windows (executed by Paul Bony) and windows by Jean Bercot, Jean Bazaine, Maurice Brianchon and Marc Chagall followed. Chagall came to stained glass late in life, but, working closely with the Reims glass-painter Charles Marcq, launched himself into a successful career in this new medium when he was over 70. From 1960 to 1965, he worked on windows for Metz Cathedral and in 1962 undertook one of his most ambitious projects, twelve windows for the Hadassah Medical Centre in Jerusalem, in which no human form could be reproduced. Each of the Jerusalem windows, representing one of the twelve tribes of Israel, employs a different colour. In his enormous Dag Hammarskjöld Memorial window in the United Nations building in New York, he used his favourite blue, in a design in which human and animal forms appear to float about in a state near weightlessness.

While the diversity of artists and styles present in a single church somewhat compromised the aesthethic integrity of the interior at Assy, the venture did a great deal to awaken the interest of leading painters in the medium of stained glass. Among the most striking of these post-war schemes are the *dalle de verre* windows of 1951 by Fernand Léger for the church of the Sacred Heart at Audincourt (executed by Louis Barillet). *Dalle de verre*, a technique developed in the 1920s by Jean Gaudin, employs the technology of the twentieth century, and is used at Audincourt to create a fresco-like wall of colour in an otherwise simple space. This new glazing method was introduced into America in 1958 by Gabriel Loire of Chartres, in the First Presbyterian church in Stamford, Connecticut (see p. 31): the combination of reinforced concrete and slab glass clouds the distinction between what is wall and what is window. Technical problems have now undermined the creation of *dalle de verre* windows, but they represent an important twentieth-century contribution to the modern glazier's repertoire.

One of the most famous painters to express himself in glass has been Henri Matisse (working in collaboration with Paul Bony). From 1948 to 1951 Matisse worked on the windows of the Rosary chapel of the

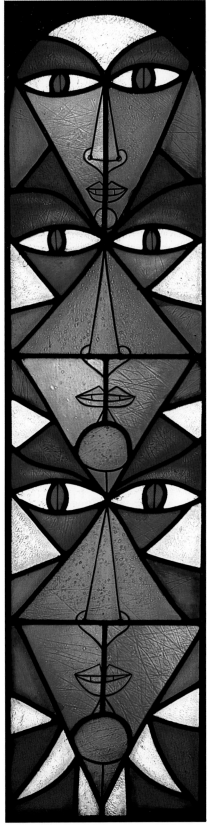

Dominican monastery at Vence (near Nice), creating windows of rich colour and simple motifs reminiscent of natural vegetal forms. For his window for the Time–Life building in New York (1952), he created a version in glass of his famous collage works, a window which now has the considerable distinction of being in New York's Museum of Modern Art.

The Church in France has been remarkably more receptive to contemporary stained glass than almost anywhere else in Europe and the active interest of the architects of the Monuments Historiques has also been of decisive importance. In cathedrals like Metz, with windows by Chagall and Jean Villon, the history of stained glass has a continuing tradition and the medium has largely escaped the threat of artistic isolation which has occurred elsewhere, particularly in post-war Britain.

Post-war reconstruction offered fewer opportunities to British stained-glass artists than to their Continental colleagues. The Arts and Crafts tradition established by Whall proved exceptionally resilient and some of the finest windows made in the second half of the century are those by followers in this tradition. Joseph Nuttgens (1892–1982), trained by the Central School of Arts and Crafts and one-time assistant to Karl Parsons, made over 300 of his own windows, in addition to executing numerous designs by other artists. Evie Hone (1894–1955), trained in glass by Wilhemina Geddes and a late member of An Túr Gloine, has long been recognized as one of the most important figures in British stained glass in the post-war period. She was strongly attracted to Rouault's luminous work in glass and as a deeply religious person (she converted to Roman Catholicism in 1937) no doubt empathized with the spirituality of his work. Above all her debt was to stained glass of the Middle Ages and, having been influenced by Cubism, she sought to evolve a new kind of figurative expression. Her most famous and influential commission was the powerful nine-light east window of Eton College Chapel (1949–52). The subject of the window is the Crucifixion and Last Supper and in this and some of her smaller commissions, Hone achieves a monumental feel, indebted to her use of strong colour and powerfully painted line. In the 1930s many artists and academics, including the stained-glass artist Erwin Bossanyi (1891–1975), sought refuge in England from Fascist persecution. Born in Hungary, Bossanyi had subsequently settled in Germany, where he became the most

**Opposite** Henri Matisse (1869–1954) collaborated with Paul and Adeline Bony in the making of this window for New York's Time-Life building (1952), reflecting his experimentation with collage. The window stands 332.5 × 139 × 1 cm (11¾ × 54¾ × ⅝ in).

**Left** *The Last Supper*, the lower half of Evie Hone's east window for Eton College Chapel (1949–52).

celebrated stained-glass artist of his day, leaving in 1934. His distinctive windows, which drew heavily on the folk-art of his homeland, display a jewel-like intensity of colour and superb craftsmanship. Examples of his work can be seen in York Minster, Canterbury Cathedral and Washington Cathedral (USA). In 1936 construction of Guildford Cathedral by Sir Edward Maufe began, to be delayed by the war and only completed in the 1960s. Moira Forsyth (1905–1991) created seven windows for it between 1940 and 1962, characterized by strong painting and fine calligraphy.

For the most part, however, these artists were creating windows for Gothic or Neo-Gothic buildings; even the new Cathedral at Guildford was in a quiet, curvilinear Gothic style. In contrast, the competition for the new Coventry Cathedral, replacing the destroyed medieval building, was won by a dramatic modern design and was intended by Sir Basil Spence to receive large areas of stained glass. Describing his wartime visit to Chartres, when the glass had been removed for safety, Spence wrote 'The Cathedral was cold and dead – like a head without eyes; and I resolved that if ever I built a cathedral, it should have singing, breathing windows.' The glass for Coventry was commissioned at an early stage in the planning; Lawrence Lee of the Royal College of Art and two of his newly graduated students, Keith New and Geoffrey Clarke, were commissioned to make the nave windows. The enormous baptistry was entrusted to John Piper (b.1903) and Patrick Reyntiens (b.1925), at that time still working on the windows for Oundle College, which Spence had seen and admired. Unlike the Oundle commis-

**Above**  A detail from John Piper's Nine Aspects of Christ in the chapel of Oundle School (Northamptonshire), executed by Patrick Reyntiens in 1955. His first commission in stained glass, it remains one of Piper's most impressive.

**Right**  The rose window for the north transept of the Cathedral and Abbey Church of St Alban, Hertfordshire. Measuring 9 m (30 ft) in diameter, the window was designed and made by Alan Younger, and unveiled in 1989.

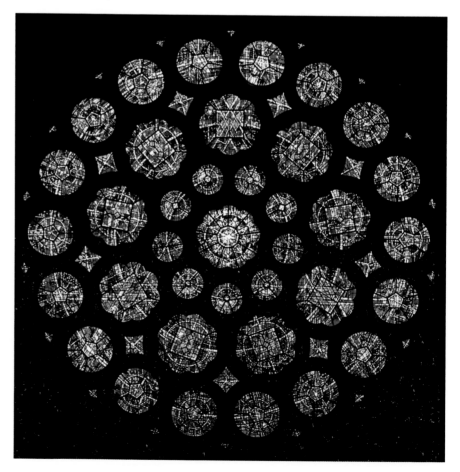

sion, with its mysterious figures of kings, the baptistry was to be abstract, in order not to compete with Graham Sutherland's great tapestry of Christ. The west window was conceived as an engraved glass screen, decorated by John Hutton (1906–78), with ethereal figures of British saints and angels. The Coventry windows remain one of the great showpieces of post-war British glass and established the reputation of the Piper–Reyntiens partnership. The same team was responsible for the controversial crown of glass (in *dalle de verre*) surmounting the Roman Catholic Cathedral in Liverpool. For the general public John Piper continues to be the best known British artist working in stained glass.

Writing in the 1990s, it is impossible to foresee what later generations will perceive to be the most important trends in stained-glass design and how the future will judge the achievements of the second half of the twentieth century. Abstract, non-figurative designs continue to predominate. The largely unpainted geometric, rectilinear approach characteristic of the post-war German school continues to exert a strong influence, in the work of the Germans Joachim Klos and Karl Traut, for example. In the abstract work of the English glass-painter Alan Younger, paint is an essential element of the window, used to modify, manipulate and control the passage of light through richly coloured glass. His 1989 rose window for St Albans

**Above** This sultry Eve is from a free-standing glass screen entitled *Adam Grabs the Apple*, made in 1990 by Bristol-based artist Rosalind Grimshaw to commemorate the Biennial Exhibition of Women's Art.

**Right** This playroom window for Mt Sinai Medical Center, New York, was designed by Albinus Elskus in 1990. Intended to brighten up a room used by children who in some cases are terminally ill, the window contains symbols of pain (the bee), health (the apple), love (the rose) and play (the squirrel).

Cathedral has demonstrated the enlivening quality of stained glass in architecture. Paint is also a key aspect in the work of the American artist Linda Lichtman, for whom motifs derived from nature recur in scratchy, textured areas of paint. A similar effect is sought in the autonomous panels by the French artist Philippe Tatre.

Over the past decade, new life has been breathed into the figurative tradition; Patrick Reyntiens' most recent work on theatrical themes teems with clowns, jugglers and characters from the commedia dell'arte. The British artist Rosalind Grimshaw regards herself as the heir of the Arts and Crafts tradition and her versatile and fertile creativity is expressed in a humane, painterly manner. In France, panels by Marie-Françoise Dromigny, teacher at the École Nationale Superièure des Arts appliqués et des Metiers d'art, depict plant and animal forms with an almost scientific accuracy. The Lithuanian-born American artist Albinus Elskus, author of one of the basic works on glass-painting techniques, achieves astonishing realism in his figurative painting on glass, mixing traditional and experimental techniques in startling combinations. In the work of relative newcomers, the Britons Benjamin Finn and Nicholas Bechgaard, the painterly and figurative tradition has talented new adherents.

The shortage of large-scale commissions has encouraged many artists to work on small autonomous panels, which in turn has encouraged experimentation with new materials and techniques. Collage techniques, fused glass and glass-appliqué (see pp. 32–3) have lent themselves to this kind of work; Thierry Boissel's untitled discs exhibited in 1990 have a delicate luminosity typical of the subtle colour effects that can be achieved by fusing. Enamels and lustres are also well suited to autonomous panels and screens. In England, Jane McDonald has used lustre to great effect, while the German artist Udo Zembok has used enamels for his small 1990 windows for the Chapelle des Camaldules at Saint-Just (France). The autonomous panels by the German-born Klaus Zimmer, now the major force in Australian stained glass, have a textured, sculptural quality and have drawn upon Aboriginal motifs and sources.

The Church continues to be a major patron, but in the late twentieth century there is also evidence that at last stained glass has begun to

**Below** The Mosque at King Khalid International Airport, Riyadh, Saudi Arabia, designed in 1983 by Brian Clarke and executed by Goddard and Gibbs.

penetrate a far wider range of architecture. A number of leading architects are now designing structures in which coloured glass is an integral part. More importantly, stained-glass artists have responded to this challenge with exciting designs. The uncompromising Brian Clarke has worked with such internationally renowned architects as Norman Foster (Stanstead Airport) and Arata Isozaki (Lake Sagami Country Club, Yamanashi, Japan), and has also created a dramatic scheme for Darmstadt's New Synagogue (designed by Alfred Jacoby) and glass roofs for the Buxton Thermal Baths and for the Victoria Quarter in Leeds. Alex Beleschenko has won many admirers for his work using float glass, the virtually flawless clear glass machine-made in large sheets, developed by Pilkington's in the late 1950s. Float glass has no character used alone, but is far cheaper than mouth-blown glass, making it an attractive material for glazing large areas. In America, Ed Carpenter has found ways of combining this cheap, functional material with other industrial glasses and more traditional materials, to

**Right** Installed in 1990, Brian Clarke's vibrant roof canopies for Victoria Street in Leeds have played an essential part in the rejuvenation of this elegant shopping thoroughfare, originally designed in 1901 by Frank Matcham, best known for his theatre designs. As in the Buxton Thermal Baths project, Clarke worked with architects Derek Latham & Associates.

create screens, skylights and windows adapted to modern settings. Using etching and aciding on large areas of colourless glass together with traditional streaky and flashed antiques, Susan Bradbury has enlivened an otherwise dead area – the lift-tower – of the Norwich Union building in Norwich with her window *Fire and Life*, covering around 140 square metres (1,500 square feet).

The twentieth century has witnessed the emergence of a major new patron of stained glass. The wealth of oil-rich Arab countries has opened up a new range of architectural opportunities and stained glass has played a prominent part in providing colour and warmth. In 1983 Clarke designed glass for the mosque in King Khalid International Airport, Riyadh (Saudi Arabia), while Alan Younger has designed the glass dome of the Royal Pavilion, Malaz Stadium, also in Riyadh. The brilliant sunshine of the Middle East permits the use of rich colour, although Muslim art cannot employ figurative motifs.

In the last decade of the twentieth century, it is clear that stained glass, a medium with a thousand years of history behind it, can look forward to the next millennium with confidence.

**Above** One of six windows by Alex Beleschenko for the ground floor of Tower Street offices in Winchester (Hampshire), installed in 1992. Measuring 2.35 m × 0.5 m, each window employs leaded glass with acid etching and painting.

# GLOSSARY

**Abrasion** The grinding away of a 'flashed' surface to reveal the clear base glass beneath.

**Aisle** The lateral vessel flanking the nave or central vessel of a church.

**Ambulatory** An aisle passing behind the east end of the central vessel of the church, connecting the side aisles of the choir.

**Annealing** The application of 'jewels' of coloured glass to the surface of white glass without recourse to leading, by painting a thick layer of glass-paint around them and firing them.

**Apse** A semi-circular or polygonal termination to the eastern limb of a church.

**Armature** The iron framework used to support panels of stained glass in Romanesque and early Gothic windows.

**Back-painting** Painting applied to the exterior surface of the glass.

**Band window** Term coined to describe a stained-glass window in which horizontal bands of full-colour (usually figurative) glass alternate with horizontal bands of grisaille.

**Came/Calme** An H-sectioned strip of lead used to hold individual pieces of glass in place. Cast in moulds in the Middle Ages, came was extruded through lead mills from the seventeenth century and soldered at the intersections.

**Cartoon** A full-scale design for a stained-glass window on parchment or paper, to include detail of painted line.

**Chevet** An apsidal east end surrounded by radiating chapels.

**Choir** The eastern arm of a cruciform church.

**Claustra (or transenna)** An early form of frame for enclosing pieces of glass or other translucent material. Made of wood, plaster, and so on.

**Clerestory** The uppermost glazed storey.

**Cut-line** A full-scale outline drawing indicating leading and guiding the craftsman in the cutting of the glass.

**Dalle de verre** A technique of window construction using small pieces of cast glass (*dalles*), 3 to 5 cm (1¼ to 2 in) thick, held in place by resin or cement. First developed in the 1920s, it was popular in the 1960s.

**Diaper** A ground covered by a pattern of a small, repeated design.

**Enamels** Metallic oxide pigments combined with flux of molten glass. Applied in solution and fired onto white glass, enamels were used extensively in the sixteenth, seventeenth and eighteenth centuries.

**Favrile** The name given to a range of iridescent glasses developed by the Tiffany glass-works, initially for tablewares.

**Ferramenta** The ironwork supporting panels of stained glass within the window opening.

**Flashed glass** A white glass to which a thin layer of coloured glass is added when the molten glass is blown. Flashed ruby (red) is the most common.

**Gothic** The architectural style prevalent from the late twelfth to the early sixteenth centuries, characterized by the pointed arch, ribbed vault and elaborate traceried window opening. Used, by extension, to refer to contemporary works in other media.

**Grisaille** Panels of predominantly white glass leaded and/or painted to form geometric or foliage designs.

**Grozing** A method of trimming glass to shape with a grozing iron, a hooked tool which leaves a characteristic 'nibbled' edge.

**Mullion** A vertical stone shaft dividing a window into individual lights.

**Nave** That part of a church west of the choir and transeptal crossing.

**Pontil** An iron rod used to gather the molten glass into a ball preparatory to blowing.

**Pot-metal** Window glass coloured throughout during manufacture by the addition of metallic oxides to the molten state.

**Quarry** A diamond or square pane of glass.

**Quatrefoil** Decoration formed of two lobes or part-circles.

**Reliquary** A receptacle to hold religious relics.

**Romanesque** The architectural style prevalent from the ninth to the twelfth centuries, characterized by rounded arches and thick walls.

**Roundel** A small (usually circular) panel, a single piece of white glass decorated with glass-paint, yellow stain and, from the later sixteenth century, with coloured enamels.

**Tracery** The stone bars forming a decorative pattern within a window.

**Tracery lights** The small compartments in the upper part of a window.

**Transept** The north or south cross arm of a cruciform church.

**Transom** A horizontal stone bar running across a window.

**Triforium** The storey beneath the clerestory, usually open to the main vessel of the church. It incorporates a well passage and the outer wall is sometimes glazed.

**Vidimus** Small-scale preparatory sketch for a window. The word means 'we have seen'.

**Yellow stain** A method of turning white glass yellow (or blue glass green), by the applications of a solution of a silver compound to the exterior surface, and firing it. Also called silver stain.

**Above** An autonomous panel showing marmosets, characteristic of the meticulously detailed glass-painting technique of Marie-Françoise Dromigny.

# USEFUL ADDRESSES

The British Society of
Master Glass-painters
6 Queen Square
London WCI

Institut del Vitrail
Granduxer 86
08021 Barcelona
Spain

Corpus Vitrearum Medii Aevi
International Technical Committee
Centre suisse de recherche
et d'information sur le vitrail
Grand-Rue 46
1680 Romont
Switzerland

Centre International du Vitrail
5 rue du Cardinal Pie
28000 Chartres
France

The Stained Glass Association
of America
6 SW 2nd Suite #7
Lee's Summit
MO 64063
USA

# FURTHER READING

The literature on stained glass is very extensive and it is only possible here to offer a selective list. All the works cited have extensive bibliographies which should be consulted. Most of the works listed are in print or else readily available.

## BIBLIOGRAPHIES

CAVINESS, M.H., and STAUDINGER, E.R., *Stained Glass before 1540, an Annotated Bibliography*, Boston, 1983.
EVANS, D., *A Bibliography of Stained Glass*, Cambridge, 1982.

## CONSERVATION AND PRESERVATION

NEWTON, R., *The Deterioration and Conservation of Stained Glass: A critical bibliography and three research papers*, CVMA Great Britain, London, 1974.
NEWTON, R., and DAVISON, S., *The Conservation of Glass*, London, 1988.

## TECHNIQUES

CENNINI, Cennino, *The Craftsman's Handbook*, trans. D.V. Thompson, New York and London, 1954.
ELSKUS, Albinus, *The Art of Painting on Glass*, New York, 1980.
FRODL-KRAFT, Eva, *Die Glasmalerei: Entwicklung, Technik der Glasmalerei*, Vienna and Munich, 1980.
REYNTIENS, Patrick, *The Technique of Stained Glass*, London, 1967.
THEOPHILUS, *De Diversis Artibus (The Various Arts)*, ed. and trans. C.R. Dodwell, London, 1961.
WHALL, Christopher, *Stained Glass Work*, London, 1905.

## SELECT BIBLIOGRAPHY

Detailed catalogues of medieval stained glass are published by the international *Corpus Vitrearum Medii Aevi*. Some national committees (notably in France and the USA) have also produced summary catalogues of stained glass of all periods. Each CVMA volume contains a list of published and proposed publications and this series is the most authoritative and comprehensive source of reference. The principal journals and periodicals dealing with stained-glass studies are *The Journal of Stained Glass* (Great Britain), *The Journal of Glass Studies* and *Stained Glass* (USA) and *Vitrea* (France).

ADAM, Stephen, *Decorative Stained Glass*, London, 1980.
ARCHER, Michael, *An Introduction to English Stained Glass*, London, 1985.
BRISAC, Catherine, *A Thousand Years of Stained Glass*, London, 1986.
BROWN, Sarah, and O'CONNOR, David, *Medieval Craftsmen: Glass-Painters*, London, 1991.
CORMACK, Peter, *Christopher Whall*, Exhibition Catalogue, London, 1980.
COWAN, Painton, *Rose Windows*, London, 1979.
CREWE, Sarah, *Stained Glass in England 1180–1540*, London, 1987.
DEREMBLE, Jean-Paul, and MANHES, Colette, *Les Vitraux Légendaires de Chartres*, Paris, 1988.
DUNCAN, Alastair, *Tiffany Windows*, New York, 1980.
ERI, Gyongyi, and JOBBAGYI, Zsuzsa, *A Golden Age: Art and Society in Hungary 1896–1914*, London and Miami, 1990.
GORDON BOWE, Nicola, CARON, David, and WYNNE, Michael, *A Gazeteer of Irish Stained Glass*, Dublin, 1988.
GRODECKI, Louis, *Le Vitrail Roman*, Fribourg, 1977 and 1984.
—— and BRISAC, Catherine, *Gothic Stained Glass*, London, 1985.
HARDEN, D.B., HELLENKEMPER, H., PAINTER K.S., and WHITEHOUSE, D.B., *Glass of the Caesars*, Milan, 1987 and 1988.
HARRISON, Martin, *Victorian Stained Glass*, London, 1980.

LAFOND, Jean, *Le Vitrail*, Paris, 1966 and subsequent editions.

LEE, Lawrence, SEDDON, George, and STEPHENS, Francis, *Stained Glass*, New York and London, 1976 and subsequent editions.

MALE, Emile, *The Gothic Image*, New York, 1972.

MARCHINI, G., *Italian Stained Glass Windows*, London and New York, 1957.

MARTINDALE, Andrew, *Gothic Art*, London, 1967.

MOOR, Andrew, *Contemporary Stained Glass*, London, 1989.

MORRIS, Elizabeth, *Stained and Decorative Glass*, Baldock, 1988.

NEWBY Martine, and PAINTER, Kenneth, *Roman Glass*, London, 1991.

PERROT, Françoise, *Le Vitrail Français Contemporain*, Lyons, 1984.

SEWTER, Charles, *The Stained Glass of William Morris and his Circle*, 2 vols, New Haven–London, 1974.

WILSON, Christopher, *The Gothic Cathedral*, London, 1990.

ZAKIN, Helen, *French Cistercian Grisaille Glass*, New York and London, 1979.

## PICTURE CREDITS

**Right**    Trained by both Patrick Reyntiens and Ludwig Schaffrath, Ed Carpenter is committed to designing for the large-scale architectural context, combining modern design and traditional craftsmanship. His work for the Green Valley Library, Henderson, Nevada, designed in 1987 and fabricated by Tim O'Neill Studios, used hand-blown glass.